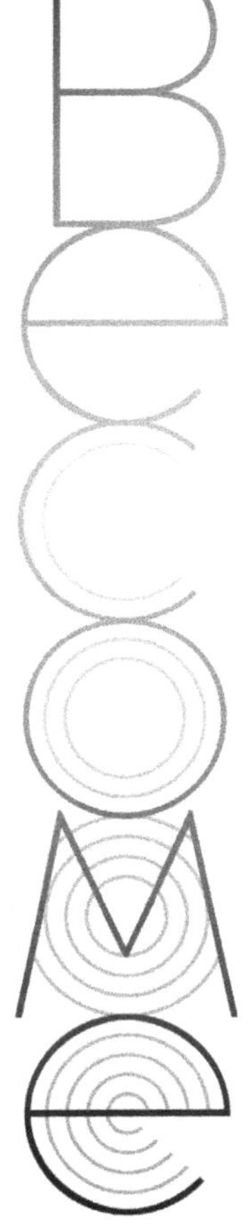

Embracing Discipleship as a Lifestyle

Sam Barber

THE FOUNDRY
PUBLISHING®

The Foundry Publishing®
PO Box 419527
Kansas City, MO 64141
thefoundrypublishing.com

ISBN 978-0-8341-4398-2

Cover design: Caines Design
Interior design: Sharon Page

Library of Congress Cataloging-in-Publication Data
A complete catalog record for this book is available from the Library of Congress.

CONTENTS

INTRODUCTION

You and I were born into a changing world. By that I certainly mean a world that is changing more rapidly than ever before. However, my broader meaning is that you and I are part of a world designed for change. Acorns become oaks, children grow into adults, and seasons pass one to another. When we pause to consider, it appears that change is built into the design of the world God created. What if our desire and capacity to embrace the Great Commission could also change?

Recently a gifted pastor used a compelling illustration as he challenged the congregation to engage discipleship as a lifestyle. He described the metamorphosis of a caterpillar into a butterfly, something many of us learned about in science class. Using his gifts as a communicator, he stoked our imaginations, saying, "If we could talk to the caterpillar, here is what we might say: 'Hey, fuzzy, little, wormlike creature. I know you can't imagine it right now, but one day you will have wings and your chubby little body will transform into one that will soar all over creation.'"[1] Of course, a caterpillar can't reason as we do, but imagining that conversation opened the understanding of all of us who listened. He likened the change required to become disciple makers to the change in the

1. Thank you, Pastor David Goodwin, for your gifts in preaching.

caterpillar. To a caterpillar, inching along the ground, flying must seem impossible, and to many believers, engaging Jesus's Great Commission feels just as out of reach.

Anyone reading this book wants to please Jesus, and most likely, we are aware that Jesus challenged his disciples and ultimately all of us to "go and make disciples" (Matt. 28:19). Our struggle is that while we understand what Jesus said, we haven't felt very successful at actually doing it.[2] This book offers hope. What if we, by the grace of God and our cooperative efforts, could become something that we aren't right now? What if we, like the caterpillar, could change into disciple makers, growing the kind of disciples who also engage in the Great Commission?

The title of this book summarizes its focus: we can *become*. We can change, and we can become disciples—the kind who follow Jesus devotedly and bring others along with us on our journey of grace. God created us with the capacity for change, and Jesus makes discipleship possible for everyone who believes. The power of God offers us a deep and lasting transformation that inevitably impacts our relationships with the people around us. Our Wesleyan-Holiness theology affirms this kind of optimism. We are convinced that God has the power to change lives and that God has offered that power to us through the redemptive work of Jesus Christ. We are not doomed to a life of "sin-repent-repeat," but rather we can know not only the forgiveness of sin but also the freedom from the necessity to sin. Like the old hymn said, "He is able to deliver thee."[3]

---

2. "Are Christians Too Busy for Discipleship Community?" Barna, February 7, 2024, https://www.barna.com/research/christians-too-busy/.

3. William A. Ogden, "He Is Able to Deliver Thee," in *Sing to the Lord* (Kansas City: Lillenas, 1993), no. 339.

We believe that what God begins in a moment, God continues for our lifetime. We are being saved and being sanctified as we walk with God. What may have begun at a youth camp or revival strengthens and grows more alive and impactful every day. What if we applied this theology to Jesus's Great Commission? What if we acknowledge that just as we can become more and more like Christ, we can also become more adept at answering his call?

We can, and that's what *Become* is all about.

I'm grateful to serve among Christ followers who share Jesus's priority of discipleship. Our denomination's mission statement is "Making Christlike disciples in the nations." Discipleship is not a program or an emphasis; discipleship is the heart of the church.[4] A healthy heart makes a healthy body possible. Likewise, healthy discipleship fuels the whole church. Said differently, a weak heart leads to a dying body, and weak discipleship leads to a dying church. This is a chilling reality to be sure, but one we must face.

In our denomination, the "journey of grace" has helped the church to grasp God's work in discipleship.[5] Let's summarize what we know. We know that God has acted first and poured out grace, drawing us, saving us, and sanctifying us. We know that Jesus stood on a mountainside and commissioned his disciples to carry on the ministry he had begun, a ministry of making disciples. We know that these were not simply historical events recorded in the Scriptures but that Jesus's intent was for all believers to carry on his ministry.

---

4. Africa Regional Director Daniel Gomis, phone call with author, August 2024.

5. We are grateful to the Board of General Superintendents and former Nazarene Discipleship International global director Dr. Scott Rainey for this global emphasis. See Dr. David Busic's book *Way, Truth, Life* (Kansas City: Foundry, 2021) for a full explanation of the "journey of grace."

The question that begs to be asked of all of us is, If we know this, why are we struggling to do it?

Discipleship authors and pastors have a host of reasons for this, but I'd like to suggest that at least two things are lacking. First, we lack clarity about how to engage the Great Commission. And second, we lack a strategy for carrying it out.

I'll address the clarity question here through a definition of discipleship. The strategy question unfolds in the ensuing chapters of *Become*.

A Definition of Discipleship

Recently I came across a news article that captured my imagination. The headline promised to reveal the word in the English language with the most definitions.[6] I was intrigued as I tried to imagine what this word might be. I was stunned to learn that the word promised in the article is the tiny word "run." It turns out that this diminutive word has 645 definitions in its verb form alone! For example, we *run* when we accelerate our walking pace, moving our legs more quickly, but we may also permit our name to appear on a ballot if we decide to *run* for office. When we use our air conditioner, we may say it is *running*, or we may be stopped by the police for *running* a stop sign. Hundreds of definitions for one little word helped me realize that often the same word can mean different things to different people or when applied in various contexts.

"Discipleship" is a word with many definitions. It seems that every conference, church, or book has a little twist on what it

---

6. "Has 'Run' Run Amok? It Has 645 Meanings . . . So Far," Pop Culture, NPR, May 30, 2011, https://www.npr.org/2011/05/30/136796448/has-run-run-amok-it-has-645-meanings-so-far.

means to be a disciple. That may not be a bad thing, but it can lead to confusion, and confusion leads to inaction.

I'd like to call us back to a clear understanding of discipleship, something we agree forms a foundation for all we will do as we become disciples ourselves and bring others along with us on that journey. This definition must emerge from the words and ministry of Jesus. The hope is that clarity around what Jesus asks of us will open up practical and achievable ways to take up the Great Commission.

History often records the first words and last words of important figures as a kind of summary of the person's life. Reading through the Gospels, it is clear that discipleship was a top priority for Jesus. His invitation to "follow me" (see Matt. 4:19) occurs at the *outset* of his ministry. The commission to go into the world and make disciples occurs near the *end* of his ministry. Do you see it? Jesus's ministry was bracketed, beginning and end, by his emphasis on disciple making. What's more, Jesus's words illuminated his ministry, day by day transforming his friends into disciples.

In our local church settings, discipleship often encompasses many things. However, whatever we do under the banner of discipleship must be built upon discipleship as Jesus himself defined it. In the words of the New Testament, discipleship is defined as following Jesus (Matt. 4:19) and making disciples (28:19) by bringing others along on our journey of following Jesus. Another way to say this that might make it more memorable to us is, "Discipleship is following Jesus and making disciples, including others in our journey of grace."

This definition emerges from the life and ministry of Jesus and results in a powerful outcome, one that should be no surprise to Wesleyans. Discipleship so defined actually pulls us toward heart holiness. Following Jesus with the kind of commitment exhibited by the first disciples helps us realize the need for God's ongoing work in us. When we begin following Jesus, we soon realize the battle within us. We want to obey but feel such a pull toward self and sin. In time we discover the need to surrender everything to Jesus and be filled with his Spirit. Indeed, the goal of following Jesus is Christlikeness by the power of the Holy Spirit. What a delight to discover that the pathway to holiness runs through discipleship!

As we follow, the pursuit of Jesus becomes more important to us than anything else. We begin to have a heart like Christ, which moves us to reach out with the love of Jesus to those in our lives. The Spirit of God always moves us to love. Just as Pentecost didn't drive the believers deeper into seclusion but propelled them into the streets, so the power of the Spirit in us moves us to engage our neighbors and friends. True to our Wesleyan roots, Christ's love compels us to reach out, inviting others along with us on our journey of grace.

To sum up, "following" looks like full surrender and the infilling of the Spirit. "Making disciples" looks like God's perfect love motivating us to bring others along with us on our journey.

One more nuance of the definition energizes the Great Commission. When Jesus stood on the mountainside and called his followers to make disciples, he spoke to them *as a group*. Inherent in the call is the reminder that we best pursue Jesus and include others when we *do it together*. We need the support and fellowship of other believers to keep us encouraged and accountable to the ministry of following Jesus and including others.

Having established a working definition, we are ready to turn our attention to a strategy for discipleship renewal in the church. How can we go from caterpillar to butterfly, from crawling to soaring in discipleship? I think this transformation only happens when you and I embrace change.

This book is a love letter to the church, but it is not written to churches. It is written to you, the Christian, the follower of Jesus. You are the church. You've heard Jesus's call to make disciples, but you've struggled to do it. And, in some cases, you've decided that discipleship isn't for you. I'd like to urge you to reconsider for at least two reasons. First, the Great Commission isn't optional. It isn't only for the "super Christians" among us. This call originated with ordinary fishermen, and it continues to us. This call is for every believer. Second, without discipleship the church exists only as a human organization slowly deteriorating into irrelevance. The church is called to make disciples, and without disciples there truly is no church.

The Layout of the Book

The chapters of *Become* are sourced from the life of Simon Peter. Using the Gospel of Mark, Peter's eyewitness testimony recorded by John Mark, we will discover Peter's journey from denier to discipler. We will also use the book of Acts and the Gospel of John to round out our discoveries.

Why Simon Peter? First, most believers see themselves in the humanity of Peter. W. Brian Shelton reminds us that while Peter is historically depicted as strong and authoritative, his "superhuman aura is balanced by a portrayal in the Gospels as perpetually imperfect."[7] Second, no one in the New Testament more beautifully embodies "becoming" than Peter. We can see his maturation from

7. W. Brian Shelton, *Quest for the Historical Apostles: Tracing Their Lives and Legacies* (Grand Rapids: Baker Academic, 2018), 89.

the Gospel's boat-jumping, sword-wielding hothead to the thoughtful, articulate innovator of the book of Acts. As Jesus promised, Simon Peter goes from fisherman to disciple maker or, to use our analogy, from crawling along the ground to soaring above. As we examine the life of Peter, we'll discover that we can do the same.

Additionally, each chapter will cover three areas. We will look first at the scriptural record for Simon Peter, highlighting in each chapter one of six principles from the story of his life. Next, we will acknowledge the need in our own lives and that of the church that corresponds to Peter's experience. Finally, we will apply what we learn from the transformation that occurs in Peter's life to our own lives for the cause of discipleship.

For English speakers, the word "become" serves as an acronym, each letter reminding us of a key step in a renewal of our passion for the Great Commission. However, even without the acronym, the principles of *Become* provide practical steps in discipleship renewal.

Finally, a word about the acronym "BECOME." As a preacher, I was tempted to use acronyms because they are memorable. However, the temptation to choose a word, and therefore a concept, because it begins with the right letter can dramatically alter the direction of the sermon. The same is true of writing. Acronyms are effective, but they cannot drive the content.

An amazing thing occurred with BECOME. I worked on the acronym as a way to help our denomination's USA/Canada Region with its Cycle of Resurgence emphasis. What I soon discovered, however, was that the words and concepts that the acronym inspired in me really express my heart for the church and discipleship. We really do need to **b**egin again. We really do need to **e**ncounter the Spirit. We really do need to **c**onnect with others. We really do need to **o**rganize our lives around Jesus's priority. We really do need to **m**ake ourselves accountable if we hope to make any progress. And we really do need to **e**ngage, to start, to take tangible steps, to change the way we've been pursuing the Great Commission.

Acronyms are great, but these priorities flow from my heart and challenge me to truly hear Jesus calling me to follow him and go and make disciples. Will you join me?

1 BEGIN AGAIN

The Importance of Simon Peter

If the Gospel writers created a promotion for beginning again, Simon Peter would be the face on the marketing materials. Even now you may be remembering some of Peter's infamous exploits as an apostle. We'll point to several of those throughout this book. Peter's explicit fallibility is one of his most endearing traits. However, a few words about the historical person of Simon Peter might strengthen our use of him as an example.

Peter's parents actually named him Simon. Jesus added "Peter," our interpretation of the Greek word for rock (Matt. 16:18). Frequently, we refer to this apostle now as simply Simon Peter. Peter had a home in Capernaum. Jesus and his friends frequented Peter's home. He had a wife and, legend records, at least one child, a daughter. Peter had a fishing business and provided for his family from the sea in what one author called a balance between "occupational hazards and starvation."[1] Peter's apostleship in the Gospels is

1. Heather, "Caught Between Occupational Hazards and Starvation," *Envision Bible World* (blog), May 19, 2018, https://www.envisionbibleworld.com/2018/05/caught-between-occupational-hazards-and-starvation/.

marked by passion, outspokenness, and a "ready, fire, aim" manner. Yet, even in his imperfections, we see in Peter a follower, a learner, and ultimately a leader.[2]

In some ways, though we're separated by more than two thousand years, he is not so different from us. The pressures of his life resemble our own. A husband, a father, a friend, a business owner—Peter had responsibilities and a meaningful existence even before he met Jesus. Knowing this endears him even more to our imaginations as we look to him as an example in this book.

We often romanticize being a disciple. What must it have been like to walk with Jesus and listen to him engage with others? We fantasize that our obedience to Jesus would have been simplified by knowing Jesus in the flesh. However, we forget that, like Peter, we are imperfect. Our faithfulness ebbs and flows. Imagining Jesus confronting our failures is far less romantic. Yet that is where we find Peter—trying and failing and then beginning again. I can relate. I think you can too.

I find at least three new beginnings in the life of Simon Peter. My hope is that by lifting these examples up, we can draw strength from them and begin again ourselves.

Peter's New Beginnings

Begin Again No. 1

Mark 1:16-18 records Jesus's call of Simon and his brother Andrew. We've read these verses so many times that the creativity of Jesus's call goes unnoticed. But imagine you are Simon. You begin your days early preparing the boat and nets. You feel the pressure of providing for your family and competing with your

2. Shelton, *Historical Apostles*, 61-66.

neighbors who have similar needs. Your world is narrowly focused on the sea, the equipment, your partners, and your existence. You work at the mercy of the weather, often well into the night, and more often than not, the need far exceeds the catch. Peter, better than any of us, intuited the weight of Jesus's call. Fishing in the first century was not for the faint of heart, and fishing "for people" (v. 17) carried connotations of a similar singular devotion.

Peter's first new beginning was the invitation to trade a life of fishing for a life of following. Sometimes I try to imagine what his wife and family thought of his new adventure. How did they survive his three-year walkabout with Jesus? Regardless, true to what we will learn about Simon, he responds to Jesus with a passionate, life-altering yes.

As we consider beginning again, I pray we are emboldened by Peter's radical obedience. He may have been "only" a fisherman, but he was smart enough to know that following Jesus was the way to go.

Begin Again No. 2

Peter begins again in dramatic fashion after his utter failure during Jesus's trial. Mark 14 records the story. Jesus predicted Peter's denial, to which Peter emphatically and true to form protested. Then while Jesus faced the inquisitors, Peter denied ever knowing Jesus. Even now I shake my head at the desperation of this moment in Peter's life. Far from judging him, my heart aches for his desperation. Imagine his utter devastation as Jesus goes to the cross. Peter is unable to make amends, and in the midst of his grief, Jesus dies. We catch a glimpse of his despondency in verse 72, where we read that as the rooster's crow faded, "he broke down and wept."

At a recent meeting in Barcelona, Spain, we were afforded an afternoon to visit the Sagrada Família, a magnificent cathedral in the heart of the city. The architecture is stunning and represents a project, still incomplete, that began in 1882. Just to the right side of the central entrance a solitary figure has been carved. He is crumpled to the ground, his sandstone shoulders bent and his face marked with the agony of a broken heart. Etched into the wall a few feet away is a rooster. The gospel came alive once again for me. Something about the sharpness of the chiseled edges of the face and the humanness of Mark's scriptural account moved me to tears as I witnessed the artist's depiction of Peter's denial and deep regret. I'm grateful that Peter's despondency didn't move him to choose the way of Judas, who in a similar state of failure took his own life. Instead, as we'll see, Peter is offered a fresh start, a chance to begin again.

The days following the crucifixion were filled with fear, grief, questions, and "too good to be true" resurrection accounts from the women. Mark's Gospel singles out Simon Peter in the words of the resurrection angel: "But go, tell his disciples and Peter, 'He is going ahead of you into Galilee. There you will see him, just as he told you'" (16:7). I like to imagine that the specific address of Peter offered him a glimmer of hope. If Jesus really was alive, Peter might get the chance to make amends. Mark's Gospel ends rather abruptly, and we look to John to finish this story.

John 21 records Peter announcing that he is going out to fish. It's unclear whether he imagines the three-year experiment with Jesus is over or if he simply needs to provide. Whatever the case may be, after a fruitless night, a stranger on the beach urges Peter and those with him to try a new technique. For reasons known only to the fishermen, they give it a try and catch so many fish that the net threatens to break. When Peter realizes it is Jesus who has called to them, he jumps from the boat and swims to shore.

I love the scene of Jesus, a fire, some bread, some fish, and these disciples gathered around. I'd love to have been there, but I'm not sure I would want to be in Peter's sandals. After breakfast, Jesus turns his attention to Peter. Three times the resurrected Jesus asks, "Do you love me?" (vv. 15-17). It is a beautiful and agonizing scene as Peter affirms his love once for each time he had denied the Lord.

Feeling the full weight of that encounter, Peter decides to begin again. He is forgiven, reinstated, reassured, and relieved, and what's more, the trajectory of his life changes dramatically. At each inquiry from Jesus, and for each affirmation from Peter, Jesus offers him a calling to feed and care for those who follow Jesus. Jesus offers Peter another chance to take up the vocation[3] of discipleship. Don't miss this: what began along the sea at Jesus's invitation to follow him is reaffirmed again, several years later, along the sea at this holy breakfast. Peter begins again to follow Jesus and embarks on a lifetime of making disciples, including others in his journey of grace.

Begin Again No. 3

The book of Acts emphasizes the ministry of Peter in the first few chapters before turning its narrative in the direction of Paul. However, in these principal chapters, Peter demonstrates yet another "begin again" moment. Acts 10 records the mesmerizing account of Peter's vision of traditionally unclean foods and God's use of that vision to open the gospel of Jesus Christ to the gentiles.

The preacher in me wants to walk you through this astonishing chapter with all its twists and turns, but I'll leave it to you to

3. "Vocation" in its original sense is from *vocatio*, the Latin word for "calling."

read for yourselves. However, we must not miss the "begin again" moment. Having lived his life as a faithful Jew, having understood his heritage to be among the chosen people of God, Peter now hears the voice of the Spirit calling him to open up the aperture of his understanding to see God's grace poured out on all people. No longer is the hope of redemption only for the children of Israel, but now Peter fully realizes that "whoever believes in [God's Son] shall not perish but have eternal life" (John 3:16*b*). God verifies this new beginning in the home of Cornelius, who is a Roman, a gentile, and in short order a baptized, Spirit-filled follower of Jesus. For the rest of his life, Peter proclaimed and discipled all those God brought to faith through his ministry—Jew and gentile alike.

Despite his failures and weaknesses, Peter was invited by Jesus to begin again. From a life consumed with making ends meet and the survival of his family, Peter was initially invited by Jesus to begin a new vocation—fishing for people. From the ugliness of betrayal and failure, Peter next was invited by Jesus to start fresh, to affirm again his love for Jesus, and to embrace discipleship's call to take care of Jesus's sheep. And from the restrictions of a traditional Jewish heritage, Peter was lastly invited by Jesus to look to the outsiders, to those often overlooked by the gospel, and to invite them to know and follow Jesus of Nazareth.

The Bible offers us the chance to witness the transformation of Simon Peter from fisherman to leader of the Jesus movement and the early church. To most of us, this story isn't new; however, what may have gone unnoticed are the times that Peter begins again. We are reminded that God's grace really is amazing, but it invites a response from all who experience it. Peter receives the call to follow, an opportunity for redemption after a terrible failure, and the chance to share the gospel with Jew and gentile alike. In each instance, Peter faced a decision. Would he go on or would he turn back? Peter chose to begin again, and his story inspires us similarly.

Application

When we enter a darkened room and flip the switch, we expect the lights to illuminate. We may forget that Thomas Edison failed hundreds of times in his attempts to create the light bulb. When we see Mickey Mouse, we may forget that Walt Disney was told by a news editor that he lacked creativity. Did you know that Albert Einstein was a poor student and faced frequent rejections as an academic before winning the Nobel Prize in Physics in 1921?

My point? No one, even those recognized as great achievers in history, had a perfect record of success. Each of these tried and failed multiple times. Importantly, Einstein, Disney, and Edison didn't let temporary failures defeat them. They didn't stop trying. They began again.

You and I know this battle as well. I have attempted to learn a second language several times. My intentions are good. The resources are adequate, but so far, I have been unsuccessful. Perhaps you have made a resolution at some point to lose weight or run a marathon, only to discover that your good intentions were overwhelmed by the challenges of the task. The painful reality is that every one of us knows what it's like to try and fail. Sometimes the failures are minimal and inconsequential, and sometimes they can be devastating.

I see a similar pattern in our spiritual lives. We can identify with Paul the apostle in Romans 7: "I do not understand what I do. For what I want to do I do not do, but what I hate I do. . . . For I have the desire to do what is good, but I cannot carry it out" (vv. 15, 18*b*). Paul's transparency here is an encouragement to us who share his struggle. I think back across my years of following Jesus. Moments of resolve sometimes melted into seasons of mediocrity. Youth camps and revivals spirited me to the mountaintops only to face the cold reality of the daily grind. When we experience discouraging times, the temptation is to give up. In our weakest moments we assume that we simply aren't up to the challenge of following Jesus. Sadly, many people walk away from their faith in disappointment or simply assume a risk-free version of religion.

The tragedy is that neither walking away nor playing it safe are options endorsed by Jesus. Choosing to follow Jesus introduces us to life in its most fulfilling expression, but it comes at a cost. Jesus talked about the narrow way and suffered death by crucifixion. Choosing to follow him isn't safe, but it is abundant and eternal. Nothing worth having comes without sacrifice; certainly, life with Jesus proves worth the sacrifice. We can say with Paul, "For our light and momentary troubles are achieving for us an eternal glory that far outweighs them all" (2 Cor. 4:17). For this reason we cannot give up or assume a nominal faith. We must begin again.

As we consider walking with Jesus and the inherent struggles, might we also consider his call to make disciples? I think our efforts to disciple others often follow a path similar to what I just described.

How many of us have heard messages preached on the Great Commission? We felt the tug of the Spirit on our hearts, urging us to get engaged in making disciples, and we set out to do it. Once again, however, we encountered the inevitable struggles of such a calling and many of us got discouraged and stopped trying. More tragically, many of us have concluded that obedience to the Great Commission is simply not for us. It's too difficult, or we imagine we aren't appropriately trained or gifted for such a thing. Like Paul, we know the good we ought to do, but we just don't do it. Please understand, I'm not condemning anyone. I've been there myself. Yet, when Jesus stood on the mountainside and commissioned his followers, he didn't make the call optional. What are we going to do about Jesus's call?

The church unintentionally offers several alternatives to embracing the Great Commission. Let me be careful here. What I list as alternatives are all good things, but they fall short of a full embrace of Jesus's call to make disciples.

For instance, church attendance is frequently the measure of the believer. Church attendance is a wonderful thing. We need the body of Christ for encouragement and corporate worship, but attending church and taking up the call to be and make disciples is not the same thing. Sincere church attendance may be a part of one's discipleship, but church attendance will not fulfill Jesus's commission.

Serving others is a popular alternative to disciple making. Again, serving is wonderful! It is the heart of Jesus, but serving alone isn't enough. Jesus was about making disciples, not just compassionately reaching out to people.

The church in our era is enamored with musical worship. There truly is something special about the power of music offered in the name of Jesus. I frequently find myself unable to utter a word or note as the tears stream down my cheeks during worship. As powerful as that is, however, it falls short of what Jesus intended as he stood on the mountainside and challenged his disciples to do as he did.

Jesus held discipleship as a matter of top priority. He defined it as we have: following him and making disciples by including others in our journey of grace. Going to church, serving others, singing and playing songs of worship, and many other church-related things can all function as a part of discipleship provided they help us to follow Jesus and bring others along with us on our journey of grace.

So, we are back to the question once again: What are we going to do with Jesus's call to "go and make disciples of all nations" (Matt. 28:19)? We've heard the call before. We've tried to be obedient before. What are we going to do?

Would you permit me to challenge you to begin again? We cannot give up or simply look the other way. Neither can we adopt a pseudo-Christianity that ignores obedience to Jesus's clear call. The commission is too important! The mission of God rests in the hands of ordinary people like us. What we do with Jesus's Great Commission, better yet, what *you* do with Jesus's Great Commission has direct kingdom impact. There is no church without disciples, and there are no disciples without disciple makers. The only option we have, it seems, is to begin again.

In Simon Peter we see the call of Christ for each of us. Like Peter, we can become consumed with survival. Despite all of our modern conveniences, we remain the busiest and most frazzled culture that has ever lived. We simply can't imagine enough margin to truly engage with our family, neighbors, or friends. How could we ever include them in our journey of grace? I believe that Jesus's Great Commission is too important to ignore despite our frantic lifestyles.[4] Jesus invites you and me to begin again to embrace the importance of his call to discipleship and to make whatever life adjustments are necessary.

Like Peter, because of our past many of us wince at the admonition to make disciples. Some of us feel unworthy to walk the journey of discipleship with others because our own track record

4. More on this subject in chapter 4.

of faithfulness is hit or miss. Others of us have sincerely tried to become disciple makers, but our efforts seemed fruitless. In either case, we need to sit with Jesus and hear him ask, "Do you love me?" When we settle the question of our greatest love, we begin to feel the Spirit's nudge toward the people around us. Consider, if Jesus can offer forgiveness and renewal to Peter whose denial may be one of the worst betrayals in history, can't he forgive our failures and false starts and help us to begin again to take up his call?

In Peter we see the scope of his witness expand. Peter broadens his outreach beyond the traditional people of God to all people. Acts 10 marks a "begin again" moment for Peter and ultimately the whole church. Perhaps God is speaking to you right now about those you've overlooked or considered someone else's responsibility. Could it be that Jesus is inviting you to take another look around you and discover where and to whom he might be calling you? I'm convinced that you are where you are for God's good purposes and that the people in your life are your mission field. May we, like Peter, open our hearts to the vision of the Spirit.

I pray that God will help you to begin again in your passion for discipleship. Perhaps two scriptures will help:

> I thank my God every time I remember you. In all my prayers for all of you, I always pray with joy because of your partnership in the gospel from the first day until now, *being confident of this, that he who began a good work in you will carry it on to completion until the day of Christ Jesus.* (Phil. 1:3-6; emphasis mine)
>
> Therefore, since we are surrounded by such a great cloud of witnesses, let us throw off everything that hinders and the sin that so easily entangles. *And let us run with perseverance the race marked out for us, fixing our eyes on Jesus, the pioneer and perfecter of faith.* (Heb. 12:1-2*a*; emphasis mine)

2 ENCOUNTER THE HOLY SPIRIT

The Gospel of Mark mentions Peter twenty-six times. In four of those, Peter asks a question or makes an observation—true to his habit of rarely keeping thoughts to himself. On the positive side, Peter's curiosity helps readers understand the story, and eleven mentions show him in a good light: he is given the name Peter by Jesus, he affirms Jesus as the Christ, and he's invited to witness the transfiguration and pray with Jesus in Gethsemane. The other eleven mentions are less flattering. Peter rebukes Jesus and is sharply corrected ("Get behind me, Satan" [8:33]), misunderstands the transfiguration, falls asleep in Gethsemane, and denies Jesus three times. This curious, outspoken disciple gets it right—and wrong. No wonder we relate to Simon Peter. We see ourselves in his story.

If the story of Peter told in Mark was the first episode of a television series, the initial references to Peter in the book of Acts might cause you to scratch your head. Mark records the angel instructing the women at the empty tomb to specifically tell Peter that Jesus is alive, but then Mark ends rather abruptly with the women fleeing the tomb in fear. Acts 1 depicts the disciples in the upper room and Peter taking leadership in the selection of an apostle to replace Judas. Peter is no stranger to leadership, but there is something different about him. He seems steady, thoughtful, and authoritative. As Acts 2 unfolds, Peter, along with all the others in the upper room, is filled with the Holy Spirit and rushes down the stairs, boldly proclaiming Jesus as the Messiah, laying the blame for his death at the feet of the Jewish religious order.

This is the same city where Jesus was tried and crucified. The same leaders still hold power. The people who shouted for Jesus's blood still occupy the houses and shops of Jerusalem. However, rather than lock themselves in an upper room in fear, Peter and these disciples shout the message of Jesus at the tops of their voices to anyone who will listen.

Encountering the Holy Spirit

The book of Mark presents Peter as inconsistent, but Acts reveals Peter as resolved. What brought about this astonishing transformation from confusion and fear to passion and power? Clearly the work of the Holy Spirit. Peter and the other apostles had two distinct experiences of the work of the Spirit in their lives. In John 20, the resurrected Jesus breathes on them and says, "Receive the Holy Spirit" (v. 22). Then on the day of Pentecost, the Holy Spirit falls on the gathered believers with a mighty wind and tongues of fire. The text says, "All of them were filled with the Holy Spirit" (Acts 2:4*a*; see vv. 1-4*a*).

Follow Peter from this point through the book of Acts and the change in him is even more evident. His brashness becomes resolve as the chapters unfold. Before his encounter with the Holy Spirit, Peter is the first to speak and frequently misses the mark. After Pentecost he is still bold but now articulate and determined. He preaches in Acts 2 and 3 with insight, and in Acts 4, without flinching he goes toe-to-toe with those who threaten his life. The puzzle pieces of who Jesus is seem to come together for him as he clearly explains the Scriptures, pointing to Jesus as the Messiah and the way to be saved. His encounter with the Holy Spirit brings out the best of God's work in him.

In the gospel accounts we might describe Peter as impetuous. "Let's go!" seems to be his theme. Following his encounter with the Spirit, however, the "Let's go" changes to a kind of sanctified "Let's find a way." His speech to the Jerusalem Council in Acts 15 recounts God's move to include the gentiles in the good news. Peter speaks with authority, but rather than appearing dogmatic, he appeals to the grace of God and points the way forward. "We believe it is through the grace of our Lord Jesus that we are saved, just as they are" (v. 11). His encounter with the Holy Spirit equips him to lead the church beyond Jerusalem, quite literally "to the ends of the earth" (1:8).

His encounter with the Spirit also alters Peter's focus. Like the rest of the disciples who occasionally vied for seats of power in Jesus's entourage, prior to his encounter with the Holy Spirit, Peter looked out for himself. We get a hint of his inward focus in Mark 10, where Peter reminds Jesus that he and the others "have left everything to follow you" (v. 28). The full expression, however, plays out in the courtyard of the high priest, where Peter chooses self-preservation over faithful witness, denying any association with Jesus.

But post-Pentecost, Peter demonstrates a move from "me" to "we." Following his powerful message resulting in three thousand new converts, Peter found himself with open hands and heart among the Acts 2:42 believers:

> They devoted themselves to the apostles' teaching and to fellowship, to the breaking of bread and to prayer. Everyone was

> filled with awe at the many wonders and signs performed by the apostles. *All the believers were together and had everything in common. They sold property and possessions to give to anyone who had need.* Every day they continued to meet together in the temple courts. They broke bread in their homes and ate together with glad and sincere hearts, praising God and enjoying the favor of all the people. And the Lord added to their number daily those who were being saved. (Vv. 42-47; emphasis mine)

The encounter with the Holy Spirit poured the self-sacrificing love of Jesus into Peter's heart, and he, in turn, poured it out on those God placed in his path. The Spirit changed everything for Peter, and the Spirit longs to do the same in us.

Application

Simon Peter's Spirit-led transformation captivates our imaginations, but do our lives reflect a similar focus? Is our discipleship empowered by the Spirit? Have we grown cold in our hearts? Has the wind and fire of Pentecost cooled to a tepid calm? To paraphrase John Wesley, it is the Spirit of God that gives life to the soul, as the soul gives life to the body. Without the Spirit, we are dead to God, and can neither think, speak, nor act for his glory. But by the Spirit, the whole body of sin is destroyed, and we are endued with power from on high.[1] Don't forget that the same people who were filled with the Spirit in Acts 2:4 were filled again in Acts 4:31. What God did then, God wants to do today.

---

1. See John Wesley, "The New Birth," in vol. 6 of *The Works of John Wesley*, 3rd ed., ed. Thomas Jackson (1872; repr., Peabody, MA: Hendrickson, 1984), 65-77.

The secret to becoming Christlike disciples isn't willpower or strategy. The means to Christlikeness is the Holy Spirit. And the work of the Spirit does more than make us holy; the Spirit makes us active! The unction of discipleship is Pentecostal power, and only the Spirit of God can bring it, sustain it, and use it to change those who cower into those with power. We've been trained to expect revival in church services and revival meetings. We've witnessed singing and preaching as conduits for the Spirit's work. Thank God for this heritage, but we mustn't lose sight of this reality: the church began when a small and weak group of people united themselves in prayer until they experienced the promised Holy Spirit. Revival broke out in the streets when the disciples encountered the Holy Spirit.

Let me invite you to encounter the Spirit by following the pattern of the Acts church.

Relational Unity

Acts 2 says, "When the day of Pentecost came, they were all together in one place" (v. 1). If any group had justification to splinter and run, it would have been this group. Their Master had been unjustly arrested, tried, tortured, and crucified. Word on the street was that his followers might be next. They could have fled, but they didn't. They stayed, and they stayed together.

The dangers of church fracture threaten the Great Commission today. Divisions over social issues, politics, and theology erode the church's witness until a watching world declares, "Look how they hate one another!" in a tragic reversal of first-century Tertullian's declaration: "See how they love one another" (*Apol.* 39).[2] Je-

---

2. English translation is from Tertullian, *Apology*, trans. S. Thelwall, in vol. 3 of *Ante-Nicene Fathers*, ed. Alexander Roberts and James Donaldson (1885; repr., Peabody, MA: Hendrickson, 1994), 46.

sus's call to make disciples sputters and fails when we quarrel and feud. We must come together around the priority of Jesus, laying down our weapons of division and taking up the mantle of discipleship. I'm convinced that God's Holy Spirit longs to see this happen among his people. What's more, God's Holy Spirit is the power behind the transformation of the church into the disciple-making force that Jesus commissioned.

Fervent Prayer

What God kindled in the fire of Pentecost, the early believers stoked with fervent prayer. Acts 2:42 demonstrates that this commitment to communion with God shaped their hearts after Christ's and lifted their vision from self-preservation to obedience to Jesus's call. The recent discipleship book *BLESS: Five Everyday Ways to Love Your Neighbor and Change the World* advocates beginning with prayer.[3] When I read the book, I began immediately to pray for the people in my life who I thought needed Jesus. I can testify that God not only formed in me a heart of love for them but also began to provide opportunities for me to engage those folks in conversation and friendship. Perhaps no activity in the church today is more overlooked than the simple act of bringing ourselves into the presence of Jesus, pouring out our hearts, listening for his direction, and obeying.

Importantly, prayer in Acts 1:14 was what led to the disciples' encounter with the Spirit, and prayer was what nurtured the work of the Spirit in their lives after Pentecost. If we want to begin again in pursuit of the call of Christ to be and make disciples, it will require an encounter with the Spirit through prayer.

---

3. Dave Ferguson and Jon Ferguson, *BLESS: Five Everyday Ways to Love Your Neighbor and Change the World* (Washington, DC: Salem Books, 2021).

Generosity

Notice how the work of the Spirit motivated generosity among them. They shared their possessions and the proceeds of their commerce. Like Simon Peter, the inward focus of self-preservation gave way to their unity around the mission of Jesus. An encounter with the Spirit moves us to generosity and in the giving of our time, talent, and treasure.

As a district superintendent (DS) in my denomination, I supported an initiative in our region to "bless our community." A leading DS on our field[4] created a program called "The Big Serve," where all the churches in our field were invited to organize service projects for the community on the same weekend.[5] We did our best to promote and plan, and when the weekend came, we were astounded at the participation. Large churches provided food and clothing for thousands; small churches ministered to the needy in their communities. Little children, teenagers, young adults, and senior citizens found a way to participate. The creativity and effort invested resulted in lasting change in our respective communities. The Big Serve was so effective that several of our churches adopted it as the name of their ministries of service.

When we encounter the Spirit of God, our perspective changes. We look up, look out, and look around for the places where God may be at work and we are moved to join him there. The stewardship of our resources changes, and we hold loosely to whatever God has given us. Everything we are and have becomes focused on the ministry to which Jesus has called us.

---

4. Note: in the Church of the Nazarene, a field is a larger area encompassing several districts.

5. Deep appreciation to Rev. Wendell Brown, who spearheaded this initiative for the MVNU field.

One of the most beautiful things about the church is that when we encounter the Holy Spirit, we can accomplish so much more together than we ever could alone. This is the plan of God. What started in Acts still works today!

Jesus's Teachings

In the tumultuous days of 2020, I made a conscious decision as a pastor to focus on the teachings of Jesus. That may sound obvious, but often preachers spend time in the other sections of the Bible. They may preach a series on the Psalms or spend a few weeks walking through the story of Israel in the Old Testament. They might dig into Paul's letters, teaching the theology of the church.

With the head-spinning reality of a global pandemic dawning on us and the concurrent social unrest in the United States, I sensed the Spirit calling the church back to the life and ministry of Jesus. What I discovered was that though we might disagree on social distancing or whether or not to wear a mask, we all needed to hear with fresh ears the teaching of the humble Nazarene. All of our church problems did not vanish miraculously—it was a challenging season—but we could find common ground. The ministry of Jesus served to unite us when the dangers of division threatened.

The early Christians devoted themselves to the apostles' teaching, which pointed to Jesus as the Messiah. We might say that the church was literally built on the life and ministry of Jesus. Again, that may seem obvious, but may I press the point just a bit? If the early church centered on Jesus, shouldn't we?

Similar to the call I felt as a pastor in 2020, one of the deep callings I feel in my role as my church's global director of discipleship is to call the church back to Jesus. I'm not alone in this emphasis; Alan Hirsch, among others, has called for a "re-Jesus-ing" of the church.[6] By this, Hirsch calls not for a minor church reform but a radical return to the life and teachings of Jesus as the anchor point for the mission of God. To paraphrase, we cannot continue an emphasis on "churchianity" but must focus instead on the devoted pursuit of Jesus Christ.

I'm convinced that calling the church back to Spirit-empowered following is a key to developing the heart of a disciple. When we hear, as Andrew, Simon, James, and John did, Jesus's words "Follow me," we must follow as they did—with full abandon. They left behind family, businesses, and convention to pursue the way of Jesus. Their encounter with the Spirit of God changed the trajectory of their lives from local fishermen to legendary church pioneers. My embrace of the life and calling of Jesus drives me not only closer to him but also outward to the people around me. A heart fully surrendered to Jesus means a heart deeply in love with the world for which Jesus died.

Table Fellowship

Following their encounter with the Spirit, the Acts believers devoted themselves to fellowship and breaking bread together (2:42). Scholars debate the significance of this language, some choosing to see a reference here to the early church's practice of the Lord's Supper. Certainly, that is not outside the realm of possibility. After Jesus's bread breaking at the feeding of the five thousand, in the company of the two travelers going to Emmaus, and during the last meal around the Passover table, none of us would be surprised if the early Christians imitated Jesus's pattern.

---

6. See Michael Frost and Alan Hirsch, *ReJesus: A Wild Messiah for a Missional Church* (Grand Rapids: Baker, 2008), and Alan Hirsch, *The Forgotten Ways: Reactivating the Missional Church* (Grand Rapids: Brazos Press, 2006), 99.

However, the language of Acts 2 doesn't demand this interpretation alone.

In fact, in Acts 2:46, breaking bread is mentioned again. Depending on how you count, I suppose, there may be three references here in just six verses for what church people usually think of when they say "fellowship." These newly Spirit-filled believers loved to be together, and frequently that gathering centered around the table.

One can imagine that the everyday activities of the followers of Jesus required their attention. They had homes, jobs, and families. But mealtimes provided an opportunity to gather with the family of faith and fill not just their bellies but their hearts with the blessing of friendship among the like-minded. Preachers often note the many times that Jesus sits at table with people in the gospel accounts. We probably shouldn't be surprised that his followers emphasized it as well.

Are your meals sanctified? What an unusual question, right? I don't have it all worked out, but there is an undeniable connection here in Acts between an encounter with the Holy Spirit and gathering around the table. In addition to table fellowship pointing backward to the life and ministry of Jesus, I wonder if Acts isn't also pointing forward. I wonder if Luke, the author, isn't inviting us to reconsider our meals as a sacred place.

There is something about sharing a meal together that changes a relationship. Maybe it's the vulnerability of eating. Does anyone else worry about the occasional meal mishap? You know, spinach stuck between the teeth, a smudge of marinara on the chin, or a stubborn crumb clinging to a beverage-moistened lip? Eating together breaks down barriers, and when those walls come down, there is space for friendship but also an opportunity for God to do something special.

Let me take this one more step. Since we all take great care to ensure that we are fed each day, what if we invited God to use our mealtimes as discipleship moments? What if our prayers before we eat transitioned from perfunctory requests for God to bless and moved a bit more toward moments of thoughtful gratefulness and appreciation for the earth, those who produce our food, and those who have prepared it? And, what if we asked God to sanctify a meal or two per week so that they transformed from simply a means of satisfying our need for food to an opportunity to gather with someone and enjoy fellowship in the spirit of Acts 2?

Sharing a meal or coffee has more than once been the occasion for conversation about faith. Jesus was notorious for dining with tax collectors and sinners, using the mealtime as a time to build relationship and nurture spiritual sensitivity. What if something so simple could help us be and make disciples? I think there is potential here for reframing something we do multiple times per day into an opportunity for disciple making.

Acts links an encounter with the Spirit to the breaking of bread and fellowship. In the spirit of obedience to Jesus's commission, we should as well.

Summary

Simon Peter's transformation from an impulsive and inconsistent follower in the Gospel of Mark to a bold and Spirit-empowered leader in the book of Acts reveals the life-changing impact of encountering the Holy Spirit. What made the difference? Pentecost. Filled with the Spirit, Peter goes from self-preservation to sacrificial mission, from fearful denial to fearless proclamation.

This same Spirit-encounter empowered the early church to live with purpose and unity. They practiced radical generosity, devoted themselves to prayer and the apostles' teaching, shared table fellowship, and made room for one another through love and grace. Their community was marked not just by spiritual fervor but by practical, Spirit-shaped action.

The message is clear: the Holy Spirit isn't a relic of the early church—it's the power we need today to become Christlike disciples and disciple makers. If we hope to live like Jesus, we must encounter the same Spirit that changed Peter's life. The invitation is still open: gather in unity, pray with expectancy, live generously, focus on Jesus, and share life around the table. When we do, the Spirit who transformed Peter will transform us too—and, through us, the world.

3 CONNECT WITH THOSE GOD BRINGS INTO YOUR LIFE

The preceding discussion about the impact of an encounter with the Spirit plunged us into the lives of the early Christians, Simon Peter included. This chapter returns us more specifically to the life of Simon Peter and his journey of connecting with those God placed in his life.

Like Peter, we must recognize that connecting with those God places in our lives has two key components. First, discipleship was never meant to be a solo journey. We need the Christian community for encouragement and accountability. For too long, the church has treated discipleship as an information-heavy pursuit, but Jesus intended something deeper—the shaping of our entire lives to reflect his. With the help of fellow believers, we learn to believe, think, and act like Jesus. Discipleship can't happen in isolation; it requires shared life. Jesus called the Twelve, in part, because the narrow way is best walked with faithful companions.

As Reuben Welch put it, "We really do need each other."[1] Peter had companions, and we should too.

Second, the invitation to follow Jesus comes with an outward-facing invitation to connect with those people God brings into our lives. If we understand drawing strength from fellow believers as the first meaning of connecting, opening our arms to our neighbors and friends and including them in our life with God is the second meaning.

Let's pause here for just a moment so that we can consider the impact of this connection. This second meaning of connection must become a priority for the church if we want to obey Jesus's discipleship call. Occasionally we can read the Scriptures and puzzle over something Jesus says, but the Great Commission is crystal clear! Like our brothers and sisters in recovery groups, every believer needs to take a fearless moral inventory of his or her engagement with Jesus's commission. If making disciples mattered to Jesus—and it did—making disciples must matter to us. The future of the church depends on it! As we will see, Peter connected with the people God placed in his life, including them in the redemptive plans of Jesus and the life of the Christian community.

Our familiarity with Jesus's call to Andrew and Peter might tempt us to overlook Jesus's intentional call to connection, but don't miss it! When Jesus called Simon to follow him, Jesus also said, "And I will send you out to fish for people" (Mark 1:17). Jesus pairs the invitation to follow with the commission to connect with others, and these connections begin immediately for Peter.

Scholars remind us that first-century Galilee was not ethnically homogenous. Peter would have had commercial interactions

---

1. See Reuben Welch, *We Really Do Need Each Other* (Nashville: Impact Books, 1973).

with people from various walks of life. Locals and foreigners alike would have utilized the fishing trade as a means of employment and sustenance.[2] Prior to Jesus, Peter knew plenty of people and interacted with them. However, Peter's decision to follow Jesus expanded his connections with people exponentially.

Mark's Gospel tells us that from the seaside where he called the fishermen, Jesus and his new companions traveled back to Capernaum for a Sabbath in the synagogue and a visit to Simon and Andrew's home. When Jesus healed Simon's mother-in-law, the whole town gathered at the door so that Jesus could heal them as well. Peter's fishing community would have been there, but also dozens of people he likely had not met. The next morning, after an early prayer session, the new disciples, still reeling from the crowds demanding to see Jesus ("Everyone is looking for you!" [1:37]), found him praying alone, only for Jesus to lead them immediately to nearby villages where even more new faces awaited them.

In just a few days, Peter has been exposed to everyone in his hometown and now sets off with Jesus "throughout Galilee" (v. 39). He's learning right away that this good news must be shared.

Only a few verses later we read that people "from everywhere" (v. 45) made it impossible for Jesus and his followers to remain anonymous. Imagine how overwhelming this must have been for Peter. Though he interacted with fishermen and merchants from around the region, he'd never known anything like this. Suddenly he is a part of the supporting cast to the most popular attraction in town. He watches as Jesus patiently teaches, listens, and heals. He sees the love of Jesus freely shared with everyone he encounters. If our portrayal of Peter as brash and impatient is true, this must have

---

2. Larry R. Helyer, *The Life and Witness of Peter* (Downers Grove, IL: InterVarsity, 2012), 24-27.

been quite the education. Mark implies that Peter and the others served as a kind of crowd control around Jesus, no doubt receiving Jesus's occasional correction for their stern rebuff of an overanxious seeker.

By Mark 3, Jesus is engaging with so many people that he has to instruct the disciples to secure a boat so he can effectively teach. I picture Peter, his powerful fisherman arms outstretched, his booming voice trying to hold the crowd back so that Jesus can climb into the boat. He's connecting with many people for sure in these opening chapters, but that connecting is about to change dramatically.

In Mark 3:13, Peter's whirlwind education escalates into hands-on ministry as Jesus commissions the Twelve not only as his companions and crowd control but now as preachers, even exercising authority over demons! Now Peter and the others find themselves listening more intently than ever to Jesus, knowing that they will be asked to preach and lead in his name. There's nothing like the opportunity to lead to make us pay closer attention to our mentors. In chapter 4, Mark records several instances of Jesus's teaching. Verses 10 and 34 depict the disciples taking Jesus aside and asking for deeper instruction, mentally preparing to carry on his ministry.

Mark 5 records the story of Jesus raising Jairus's daughter from the dead. In verses 37-40, Jesus removes everyone from the room except Peter, James, John, and the girl's parents. In the midst of this intimate scene, Jesus takes the little girl by the hand and raises her back to life. She gets up and begins walking around! A miracle to be sure, but also a lesson in connection for Peter and the others.

In the midst of the Jairus story, Jesus encounters a huge crowd and a woman who has been subject to bleeding for twelve years. Jesus has time not only to listen and bless the house of Jairus but also to attend to this woman, an outcast due to her ceremonial uncleanness in the culture. Peter has plenty of learning still ahead, but if we fast-forward his story just a bit, we can find him in Acts 3, hurrying to the temple at the time of prayer when he is stopped by a lame beggar. Prayer, as we've mentioned, was a priority for the early church, but Peter finds time to listen, speak to, and heal the lame man, taking him by the hand just as Jesus did with Jairus's daughter. I have to imagine that the Jairus encounter as well as the encounter with the bleeding woman was in his mind as he took the time to connect with the temple-court beggar.

Mark 6 continues the theme of connecting with others as Jesus sends the Twelve out two by two to preach, drive out demons, and heal in his name. Peter is now a long way from his fishing business. He's watched Jesus closely, literally rubbed shoulders with hundreds of people from the region surrounding Galilee, and now finds himself preaching, teaching, and healing in the name of Jesus. His decision to follow Jesus has led inevitably to a hurting world.

Much has been written about Jesus's "inner circle" of Peter, James, and John. This subset of the Twelve experienced some things with Jesus that the others didn't. One of those instances is Jesus's transfiguration in Mark 9. What's intriguing about this moment is that it demonstrates that while Peter has made great strides in connecting with those God placed in his life, he hasn't quite mastered the skill.

When Jesus reveals his glory alongside Moses and Elijah, Peter suggests building shelters to remain with these heroes of the faith. Even Mark observes that Peter "did not know what to say, they were so frightened" (v. 6). But God speaks, and Jesus quickly leads them down the mountain and back into ministry. Peter's idea to stay wasn't just a passing comment—it had missional implications. As R. T. France notes, Peter may have wanted to "institutionalize" the vision, misunderstanding that Jesus's mission was not to remain in glory but to go to the cross. Immediately, they rejoin the other disciples amid a crowd disputing over the disciples' failure to heal a demon-possessed boy. The mountain showed Jesus's glory; the streets revealed his mission. When Jesus heals the boy, the disciples again pull him aside, aware of how much they still have to learn.

If you're like me, you find comfort in Peter's mistake. Even this disciple who walked so closely with Jesus missed the mark. There is grace here for the church, but like Peter, we cannot restrict our strategizing to personal mountaintops with Jesus. Jesus's mission has always been discipleship, and connecting with people is a must.

Peter's world and his role expands in Mark's Gospel, revealing Peter's successes and failures, but the most profound and far-reaching expression of connection occurs in Acts 10. I'll summarize the account here.

Acts 10 reads like a well-written novel. Cornelius, Peter, the angel, and other supporting characters elevate the story to reveal Peter's biggest connecting challenge. Here we see this growing disciple literally befriend an outsider that God brings into his life. Notably, this is post-Pentecost Peter. He's been cleansed and empowered by the Spirit. Pay attention, Church! This is for us.

Cornelius is a devout Roman centurion, a rarity in Jesus's time to be sure. In a vision, God instructs Cornelius to send men and bring Peter to Cornelius's home. Like a great television show, this story is off to a fast start. The men sent by Cornelius start off on their journey to find Peter.

Meanwhile, Peter, weary and hungry in the afternoon, retreats to the rooftop of Simon the Tanner's home for a nap. In these moments God elevates the call to connect for Peter, for the church, and ultimately for all of us. Peter falls into a trance where he is invited to eat animals that are strictly forbidden in Jewish law. Initially, Peter recoils at this notion, being a faithful Jewish man. However, God speaks to Peter, saying, "Do not call anything impure that God has made clean" (v. 15). Three times Peter sees this vision, and just as he awakens, there is a knock at the door of his host. The men from Cornelius have arrived, and they're asking for Peter.

The Spirit speaks to Peter, foreshadowing his inevitable resistance as a faithful Jew to what is about to happen: "Do not hesitate to go with them, for I have sent them" (v. 20). Peter hurries down the steps and speaks to the men. We can't miss the importance of this moment. Here is Peter, a faithful Jewish man now being invited to enter the home of a gentile, something the law forbids. What's more, this particular gentile represents the oppression of Rome over the Jewish people of the region. As Bible readers, this moment is the climax of this episode.

In a moment that reveals not only Peter's hospitality but also his growth as a follower of Jesus, Peter invites these guests into Simon's home. The next day he sets out with them to visit Cornelius. The law built walls between Jews and gentiles, but God is up to something new. The story now unfolds more rapidly. Peter shares the core message once he arrives at Cornelius's home and greets all who are gathered there. The message is that God's plans for redemption and new creation include all people, not just the historic people of God. Cornelius, his family, his servants—all hear the good news that Jesus came for everyone. While Peter is still speaking, the Holy Spirit falls on those hearing the message, and they are baptized.

All that Jesus had taught Peter, all that he had modeled in his presence, Peter now gathers up and pours out on Cornelius and friends. What a journey Peter has had! Like Jesus, he prayed. Like Jesus, he obeyed. Like Jesus, he opened his heart and his hands to the stranger. Like Jesus, he went where Jewish tradition said he shouldn't go. Like Jesus, his connection with those God brought into his path not only changed their lives but also swung wide the gates of the kingdom to all people—you and me included.

Application

When we began this chapter, we discovered the dual nature of connection. We emphasized the importance of connecting with other believers for encouragement and accountability. We need each other. Walking the way of Jesus is challenging. I'm convinced that "solo Christianity" accounts for much of the spiritual anemia in our churches. God intends our faith to be lived out together.[3] However, an equal, if not more desperate, need lies in our hit-or-miss efforts to connect with those whom God places in our lives. I fear that our love for the church and the fellowship we find there with like-minded sisters and brothers numbs us to the call to "go and make disciples." Certainly, there may be a variety of reasons for our tendency to prefer interactions with the like-minded, but Jesus didn't say much about preference in the Gospels. He was clear about his commission.

3. See Sam Barber, *A People of Grace: Becoming Disciples Together* (Kansas City: Foundry, 2023).

A few years back, in an effort to help our congregation understand this, I invited our church board, a group of fifteen people, to join me on the platform. I instructed them to form a circle and join hands. They did exactly as you would imagine. They turned toward one another, exchanged a few whispers and grins, and then took one another's hands and peered over at me. I talked for a few moments about the importance of connecting with one another on the journey of faith. Frankly, no one was shocked at this visual representation of Christian community.

Then I asked them to do something else: stop holding hands, turn 180 degrees, and then rejoin hands. Again, after a few whispers and grins, they accomplished the simple task. They still formed a circle, they were still connected by holding hands, but now instead of facing one another, they faced outward. This, I believe, must become the posture of the church together, connected, mutually supporting one another, but facing outward to a hurting world where people are desperate for hope.

We cannot repeat Peter's transfiguration mistake. The safety of the mountaintop with Jesus must always result in connecting with those in the valley. If Jesus's call to Peter and the other fishermen carried an explicit call to connect ("I will *send you out* to fish for people" [Mark 1:17; emphasis mine]), we cannot imagine that the call has somehow changed. Jesus still sends us out to fish for, to connect with, people. The call to follow Jesus always includes a call to connect with others. Lord, give us ears to hear!

As I travel the country, participating in discipleship conventions and workshops, I often hear church people lament that they don't know their neighbors. I can relate. For many years I found plenty to keep myself busy, much of it involving people, so that when I finally had some time to myself, I wanted to keep that time for myself. It's taken me a long time to learn my lesson, but the problem I had with knowing my neighbors wasn't a problem with them or even that I was being selfish with my time. The problem was that I was too busy, leaving little or no margin in my life. I had virtually no energy for anything or anyone outside of my work. One of the tragedies of modern Christians is that we regularly violate the spirit of Sabbath. We work, play, and waste time too much and have nothing left for those around us.

In recent years I have tried to build more margin into my life. I need time to unplug not only for my health and well-being but also so that God can "interrupt" my life with some divine appointments. God is already at work in the lives of the people I call neighbors and friends. From time to time, God needs us to join him. I can't join him if I don't plan to have time.

Importantly, Jesus used the fishermen's profession to frame their call. Jesus was not oblivious to a fisherman's life and community. When he invited these men to fish for people, they imported their understanding of fishing to connecting with people. They knew plenty about hard work, knowing when to fish and where, and that there were no guarantees of success. When they imported this experience over to connecting with people evangelistically, their mentality stabilized their ministry.

As we consider turning our lives in Christ 180 degrees to face outward, I wonder if God might also desire to use our professions as means of connection? God may call some of us away from our professions, as he did Peter and the others. However, God will more likely use our professions as conduits to share his love, if we're open to it. Chances are you interact with people regularly who don't yet follow Jesus. I'm convinced that Jesus wants to use those interactions, those relationships, as means to share his love. Think of it like this: the connections in your life matter to God. Are you willing to invite God into your profession?

When I was a college student, our chaplain invited a plumber to speak in chapel. I never forgot the story of this godly tradesman who surrendered his profession to Christ, using his encounters with customers as open doors for sharing the love of Jesus. Hundreds of people in that community heard about God's love, many of them turning their lives over to Christ as a result of this plumber's witness. A few weeks ago, I was chatting with a church member from that area and brought up his name. "Oh yes!" she replied. "Not only do I know who that is, but I'm in the church today as a direct result of his influence." God uses fishermen and plumbers, as well as pastors, teachers, nurses, attorneys, and anyone else who reimagines his or her profession as a place where Jesus wants to work.

Let's not overlook the people closest to us in our discipleship efforts. A simple grammar lesson from the Great Commission helps us here. When Jesus says, "Go and make disciples of all nations" (Matt. 28:19), the grammatical form is not an imperative. This sentence isn't a command but an everyday invitation. A more literal translation of the commission is usually rendered, "As you go, make disciples." I see a powerful lesson here. Making disciples isn't so much a special emphasis as it is a function of our everyday lives. Wherever we go, whomever we meet, whatever the circumstances, Jesus is already present and working. I suspect that with our awareness of this truth, God may open new doors to share his love, "as we go."

Before we move on to the next letter in BECOME, let's try to summarize this chapter. In the first place, Peter's journey from fisherman to apostle models the dual nature of connection. The call to follow Jesus is inseparable from the call to connect with others. God invites all believers to a life of communal discipleship and everyday mission.

4 ORGANIZE YOUR LIFE AROUND JESUS'S PRIORITY

Without genealogy or birth narrative, the Gospel of Mark begins with this hopeful proclamation: "The beginning of the good news about Jesus the Messiah, the Son of God" (1:1). A quote from the prophet Isaiah frames John the Baptizer as a forerunner to the Messiah, and his prophetic message makes it clear that God is up to something big. Jesus then appears and is baptized, emerging from the waters and going into the wilderness, a clear connection to the story of Moses, Israel's first deliverer. Mark highlights this connection as a reminder to his readers that God has been faithful and is preparing to satisfy their centuries-old longing. When Jesus begins to preach, his message is the announcement that God has chosen to begin this deliverance through his own life.

God's abundant grace radiates at center stage. God the Great Initiator has chosen to act in the person of Jesus, interrupting history's plodding demise with the new creation. Jesus begins immediately to enact his strategy for renewal. Walking along the Sea of Galilee, Jesus issues a simple yet transformational call to two fishermen: "Come, follow me, . . . and I will send you out to fish for people" (v. 17).

Simon Peter, alongside his brother Andrew, responds to that call. Mark records it this way: "At once they left their nets and followed him" (v. 18). Don't let the brevity of that statement undermine its significance. In that moment, Peter began the journey of organizing his life around Jesus's top priority: making disciples.

Scholars remind us that the decision to leave behind his nets was not merely a change in Peter's occupation; it was a radical shift in his life's direction. For Peter, as for all first-century fishermen, fishing was more than a job. Peter likely inherited his boat and fishing business from his father. Imagine the weight of walking away from your family legacy. Similarly, Peter's identity was intertwined with his life as a fisherman. What would his new identity be? He walked away from a reliable income for himself and his family. Should we presume his extended family cared for his wife and children while he followed Jesus? We mustn't permit our familiarity with Peter's story to soften the magnitude of his decision. Peter risked everything to follow Jesus. This call was not an invitation to a part-time religious engagement. It was a call to organize his entire life around Jesus and his ministry.

Peter's new life was anything but static. As detailed in the last chapter, Peter began immediately to follow Jesus throughout Galilee and Judea. Sometimes when I'm teaching about this and trying to convey the immediacy of Peter's obedience, I say, "Peter's sandals are still wet, and he still smells like the docks, but he takes off on this journey with Jesus." He followed Jesus throughout Galilee and Judea. He heard the teachings, saw the miracles, and witnessed the moments of divine glory. Peter boldly tells Jesus, "You are the Messiah" (8:29), but even then, he still has much to learn about what it means to follow Jesus fully.

The turning point comes after the resurrection. In Acts, Peter reemerges, not as a hesitant follower, but as a bold proclaimer of the gospel. He preaches at Pentecost, and thousands respond. He heals the lame, confronts the religious power brokers, and faces persecution with unshakable faith.

Aside from one account in John 21, the famous breakfast where Jesus asks Peter, "Do you love me?" (vv. 15-17), it appears that Peter never returned to the family business. When Peter laid down his nets on the shores of Galilee, he never looked back. He organized his life around the call of Jesus. His livelihood, family legacy, and personal ambitions—all became subject to Jesus's call to discipleship. His transformation from fisherman to disciple maker to church leader required a complete reorganization of his life around Jesus's top priority.

Organizing Our Lives around Jesus's Priority

What are we to do with Peter's example?

I've noticed a new wrinkle in the ever-present safety briefings aboard airplanes these days. I'm not sure when it started, but now in the spiel about what to do in "the unlikely event of a water evacuation," the flight attendants caution fliers to "obey crew member instructions and leave everything." The thought of leaving behind my laptop, phone, and personal belongings always feels uncomfortable in that moment. I try to imagine how quickly I could scoop them up and then jump out of the emergency exit! Silly, I know.

Have you tried to imagine yourself as Andrew or Simon, toiling away at the family trade when Jesus appears and calls you to radically organize your life around him and his priorities? Would you be ready to go, leaving behind family, livelihood, and heritage?

Sometimes, even today, Jesus calls in this way. Our missionary and pastor friends often have stories of walking away from family businesses or lucrative careers in obedience to Jesus's call. However, Jesus's call is not reserved for pastors and missionaries alone. It's tempting to read Peter's story as an inspiring biography from an ancient era, but to do so would be to miss the point entirely. Jesus's call to "follow me" is not reserved for first-century fishermen or just pastors and missionaries. It is the call for every follower of Jesus in every generation.

Yet in our current church context, this radical organizing of life around Jesus's call to discipleship is not as common as it should be. Believers in our churches believe the gospel, love the church, and even admire those who devote themselves fully to ministry. But when it comes to aligning our day-to-day lives with Jesus's top priority—making disciples—many of us feel more like spectators than participants.

Perhaps if we name and confront some common obstacles to organizing our lives around Jesus's priority, we can make some progress.

Obstacles to Organizing

Super Christians

Somewhere across the centuries since Jesus and the Twelve, the church has developed a two-tiered model of Christianity. We've become convinced that there are "regular Christians" and that there are "super Christians"—pastors, missionaries, seminary professors. The serious Christians are the ones who really make disciples. The rest—the regular folks—attend church, volunteer occasionally, maybe even give some money, and just try to live morally upright lives. I suspect that sounds all too familiar.

The problem is, in the New Testament there is no such division. The Great Commission in Matthew 28 was not given to a class of professional religious leaders. It was given to ordinary followers of Jesus—some fishermen, a tax collector, even a former zealot. Jesus was not commissioning experts; he was empowering followers.

The tragic result of this "discipleship-optional" mindset is that many churches are filled with people who love Jesus but are not organizing their lives around his mission. They are busy, sincere, and spiritually hungry, but they feel uncertain, even unqualified, to live as disciple makers.

Here is a moment to remember the theme of this book. Like the caterpillar, we can become. We can change into the thing God designed with God's help. Don't lose sight of that potential.

Programs over People

Another problem we face in our churches right now is an unintentional priority of programs over people. In many local congregations, the calendar is full, but the mission of making disciples is drifting. Ministries multiply, events are planned, and programs are often well executed. But digging deeper, we discover that few people are actively organizing their lives around making disciples. This is not a polemic against programming. Well-designed and implemented programs help the church, but we must recover the foundation upon which the programming is built and evaluated. The purpose of a program is to help a person follow Jesus and then from there learn to bring others along on the journey of grace.

Discipleship isn't only a class we take or a series we complete. Discipleship is a way of life. Discipleship is following Jesus so closely that what matters to Jesus begins to matter to us. Jesus came "to seek and to save the lost" (Luke 19:10). The result of following Jesus in this way always pushes us outward to people who don't yet know him. When churches rely more on programming than on relational disciple making, spiritual growth becomes shallow and discipleship passion dims.

Simon Peter didn't become a disciple maker through a curriculum. He learned by walking with Jesus. He watched how Jesus taught, how he interacted with people, how he loved, and how he led. Jesus didn't have a classroom. What he had was a movement fueled by ordinary people who decided to organize their lives around Jesus's call to be and make disciples.

Distraction

The biggest obstacle we face when organizing our lives around Jesus's priority is distraction. Despite the promises of technology to speed up our work and permit more time for rest, we now work more quickly but pack our free time with even more busyness. We live in the most distracted generation in history. Technology has given us incredible tools, but it has also made deep, intentional relationships more difficult to maintain.

Research tells us that Americans check their phones ninety-six times per day on average. Phone checking alone interrupts us once every ten minutes, and that is only one disruption in our lives. Seventy percent of professionals admit to checking email regularly outside of work hours. Add this to the reality that the average person makes over thirty-five thousand decisions per day and it's no wonder we're exhausted. We consume over five times more data per day (seventy-four gigabytes) than we did just fifteen years ago. In fact, we spend just fifteen minutes per day in uninterrupted thinking or relaxing without distractions. Church attendance, volunteerism, and even personal friendships are all on the decline. The World Health Organization now considers burnout to be an "occupational phenomenon," and it affects 77 percent of the United States workforce.[1]

Even well-intentioned church members find their schedules packed with good things that crowd out important things. Our calendars are filled with commitments, but few of them reflect Jesus's primary command to make disciples. Like Martha in Luke 10, we are "worried and upset about many things" (v. 41), all the while missing opportunities to connect with those God has placed in our lives.

I don't mean to villainize technology or suggest that we shouldn't work hard and stay busy. However, it seems clear to me that without a real effort to organize our lives around Jesus's priority, we are unlikely to engage discipleship in any meaningful way. We just don't have time! Perhaps the issue isn't really one of rebellion as much as misalignment. We have not organized our lives around Jesus's top priority. We have asked him to fit into our routines rather than allow his mission to reshape them.

We believe that the Scriptures call us to holiness of heart and life, but holiness is about more than personal purity. Holiness is about aligning every part of our lives with the will of God. Jesus made clear that God's will includes making disciples of all nations. If we hope to pursue Jesus's command, we will need to bring our distractions under his lordship and invite his Holy Spirit to help us organize our lives around discipleship.

---

1. "Burn-Out an 'Occupational Phenomenon': International Classification of Diseases," World Health Organization, May 28, 2019, https://www.who.int/news/item/28-05-2019-burn-out-an-occupational-phenomenon-international-classification-of-diseases, and "Workplace Burnout Survey—Burnout without Borders," HealthManagement.org, June 23, 2024, https://healthmanagement.org/c/hospital/Post/workplace-burnout-survey-burnout-without-borders.

Of the chapters in this book so far, this one, I think, will require the most out of us. Any of us can pray and find the help of God to *begin again*. God's astounding generosity means that the Spirit is always ready to *encounter* us wherever we are. *Connecting* with others is hardwired into our creation. God made us for relationship. But *organizing* our lives around Jesus and his priority is tough. Everything in our lives asks us for more—more time, more finances, more attention. Without the help of God, we can find ourselves quite far from where we intended to be. The forces of culture are so strong.

What's more, this is nitty-gritty stuff. We need to consider simple things such as what time we wake up each morning and what we do with those minutes or hours before we start our day's work. We need to consider how we work, what we do during breaks, and whether the investment of time and energy is worth a few more dollars. We need to evaluate our "free time" and that of our children. We seem determined to raise our kids to be even busier than we are as we hustle from school to dance to soccer to piano, and to other activities.

Truly following Jesus will never come naturally. Jesus even promised us a narrow road and our share of trouble in life. Likewise, including other people on our journey of grace will also be a challenge. We scarcely have time for acquaintances, let alone deep friendships that might result in spiritual conversations.

We cannot ignore the radical nature of this call to organize our lives around Jesus's top priority. Jesus said several things in the Scriptures that leave me scratching my head in confusion, but the Great Commission isn't one of them. I hear him. I know what he means. I know that to truly follow him I have to embrace this call.

The Spirit

Thankfully, we are not alone in this work. The same Jesus who called Peter to drop the fishing nets and follow him is still calling us today. The same Spirit who empowered Peter to stand boldly at Pentecost empowers us today. In Acts 1:8, Jesus told Peter and the others, "You will receive power when the Holy Spirit comes on you; and you will be my witnesses." Like you, I need the work of the Spirit to help me embrace the call of Jesus. I've never been busier than I am right now, yet my friends and neighbors still need Jesus. Even as I write these words, I sense the Spirit asking me what kinds of changes I will make to better organize my life around the call of discipleship.

Here's what I know: the early church was not large, wealthy, or politically powerful, but it was full of people whose lives were radically reorganized around the mission of Jesus. The Spirit still works in that way today. Wherever men and women surrender to Jesus's priority and commit to a life of discipleship, the Spirit brings life and power. The same power that draws, saves, and sanctifies makes discipleship a reality.

Organized for Discipleship

As mentioned earlier, my denomination has rightly identified its mission: "Making Christlike disciples in the nations." This mission resonates because it not only sets the course for the denomination's resources and programming but also locates every person associated with the church in Jesus's mission of discipleship. But if this mission is to be more than words, it must shape how we live. It must affect our schedules, our spending, our conversations, and our priorities.

To organize our lives around Jesus's top priority means we must recalibrate. Like Peter, we must leave behind the nets—the comfort zones, routines, and lesser pursuits that keep us from full participation in the mission.

We must ask, what would it look like if my family life was shaped around disciple making? What if my vocation became a platform for gospel influence? What if my church stopped asking, "How many are attending?" and started asking, "Who is discipling whom?"

These are the questions that lead to transformation. These are the questions that create a culture of discipleship, one life at a time.

Personal Application—from Knowing to Becoming

We've seen how Simon Peter's story illustrates Jesus's call to organize our lives around disciple making, and we've explored why we must reclaim this calling in our current moment. But none of this will matter unless it moves from our heads to our hearts—and ultimately into our habits.

Discipleship isn't simply something we understand. It's something we do. Regardless of our relative successes or failures along the way, we can become engaged in Jesus's call to discipleship if we'll organize our lives around it.

Organizing and Surrender

Before Peter could follow Jesus, he had to drop his nets. That moment wasn't just symbolic—it was practical. Fishing was Peter's livelihood, his identity, and his security. But when Jesus called, Peter left it behind to pursue something greater.

What are the "nets" in your life that keep you from following Jesus fully? Is your frantic schedule a "net" that you need to drop?

Are you tied up in fear as you consider Jesus's call? What if you believed you could lay that down and follow Jesus? Are you addicted to comfort or control? Do you feel anxious when these things are threatened? Does your life plan hinge on your success? What if your life plan was built instead on surrender?

Occasionally, I reflect on the times Jesus, a carpenter by trade, instructed Peter and the others on how to fish. I'm human, and I think I might have thought, "Oh, you know fishing, do you? Maybe you should go make a table or something and leave the fishing to us." In Luke's account of the calling of the first disciples, Jesus instructs Peter to put out into deep water and let down the nets for a catch. Peter is reluctant after having fished all night, but his surrender is evident in Luke 5:5: "Master, we've worked hard all night and haven't caught anything. But because you say so, I will let down the nets." Peter had to surrender his expertise and trust Jesus. The passage concludes with Peter and the others bailing water from the boats so laden with the catch that they were sinking. Peter was ready then and there to surrender his fishing life and organize his priorities to match Jesus's. To organize your life around Jesus's top priority, you have to reorder what matters most. That begins with a willingness to say, like Peter, "Because you say so, I will" (v. 5).

Discipleship always starts with a yes to Jesus.

Organizing Our Priorities

We cannot follow Jesus on autopilot. Intentionality is essential. When Peter followed Jesus, he didn't just add a weekly appointment to his calendar; he entered into a relationship that affected every aspect of his life.

Most of us are not called to leave our careers the way Peter was, but we are called to leverage our lives for the kingdom. That means making space—on our calendars, in our homes, and in our heart—for disciple making.

What are some simple ways we can adjust our priorities starting now?

Evaluate your weekly schedule. What gets the most time and energy? What would it look like to give the best of your week—not the leftovers—to spiritual growth and intentional relationships? What if you consider applying the tithe principle to your time?

In the Scriptures, a tithe is a tenth of our income designated as an offering to God. Consider this: if you work a forty-hour week, a tithe of your work time would be four hours. What if you used your calendar to identify four hours in your week that you could give to forming deep relationships with friends? What if you used those four hours for making a meal and then inviting a neighbor over to share it? What if you spent an hour each day for four days prayer walking in your neighborhood and welcoming casual interactions with those nearby? Be creative and imagine what a little intentionality might do for your discipleship.

Another practice might be to simplify. Not everything that is good is necessary. Some commitments need to go so better ones can take their place. This is not a new idea. In fact, simplifying is one of several time-honored spiritual disciplines, like fasting, that can awaken our hearts to God's voice. Simplifying, however, is of particular value to us in a culture overrun with activity and distraction. To get started, consider cleaning out a closet and sharing the extra clothes with a friend in need or a shelter. Go through your pantry and create some boxes of imperishable food to share. Evaluate your weekend schedule. Start with one weekend day per month and truly practice sabbath. Unplug the technology, turn off the television, get outside and invite God to speak to you in refreshing ways. Consider what unnecessary habits have crowded your schedule, and jettison one or two to make space for relational discipleship.

Prioritize presence. Disciple making is relational. It requires unhurried time, active listening, and shared life. Start small—a meal a week, a regular walk, a weekly check-in with someone you're investing in.

Follow Jesus in Real Life

It's easy to romanticize Peter's journey, but don't overlook his obvious humanity. His discipleship journey wasn't perfect; it was messy. He failed often, misunderstood Jesus regularly, and even denied him publicly. But Peter kept showing up. He kept following. He kept trusting that Jesus wasn't finished with him. As we've seen, after Pentecost Peter's effectiveness increased dramatically.

That's what disciple making often looks like: flawed people walking together toward a perfect Savior with the help of the Holy Spirit.

Don't wait until you have all the answers or feel "ready." The Great Commission is not a command to perfect performance; it's a call to obedient participation.

What if you started today by asking God the following:

- Who is one person I can invest in spiritually?
- Who can I invite into a deeper walk with Jesus?
- Who can I encourage, challenge, or simply walk beside?

Discipleship happens in ordinary conversations, over coffee, during shared struggles, and through prayerful presence.

Invite Others to Imitate You as You Imitate Christ

Paul's words in 1 Corinthians 11:1 may seem bold, but they capture the heart of discipleship: "Follow my example, as I follow the example of Christ."

Peter did this with John Mark. The Gospel we are drawing from for this book is Peter's version of the Jesus story shared with Mark, who recorded it for us. Peter shared his experiences, his failures, and his insights, and Mark wrote them down. Our stories probably won't be written up in a timeless book, but your story—your victories, doubts, and daily obedience—can impact others. I'm convinced that no experience is ever wasted. God is a redeemer, and he takes even our worst moments and uses them for his good purposes as we surrender them to him.

You don't have to be perfect to disciple someone. You just need to be available, authentic, and anchored in Jesus. Some of our most powerful witnessing can occur when we face hardships. Friends and family are often watching to see if what we profess is true even when things are challenging.

Often people who want to disciple feel inadequate because they aren't Bible experts. Honestly wrestling through the Scriptures with a friend is good discipleship. Pray for God's guidance, ask for help, and read a book together until you find the answers you seek. Discipleship doesn't require expertise; it requires authenticity.

Let's be fully transparent. Try as we might and even with the help of the Spirit, sometimes we fail. We mess up. Remember, we're in good company with the apostle Peter. What should we do then? We confess our shortcomings and repent. This is the journey of following Jesus, and in order to be authentic, we can even share this portion with those on the journey with us.

These are the moments that form disciples.

Organize Your Life around Jesus's Mission

Let's make this practical. If Jesus's top priority is disciple making, then it must become ours as well. Consider these reflection questions and action steps:

Reflection Questions

1. What are my true priorities right now? What do my calendar, budget, and conversations reveal?
2. Who am I currently discipling—or who could I begin investing in?
3. What fears or excuses are holding me back from fully embracing this calling?
4. Where can I simplify my life to make more space for mission?
5. What rhythms or habits would help me stay focused on disciple making long-term?

Action Steps

- Pray daily for one person by name whom you can disciple.
- Schedule intentional time each week to invest in a relationship with spiritual purpose.
- Join or start a small discipleship group that meets regularly and practices accountability.
- Look for everyday opportunities—at work, in your neighborhood, or through your church—to model and share your faith.
- Commit to being a learner. Disciples make disciples, but they also remain disciples themselves.

The Legacy You Leave

Peter didn't know that his decision to follow Jesus that day on the shore would impact the world. He simply said yes, day after day. And through his obedience, the gospel spread, the church was born, and lives were transformed.

Your life can have that kind of impact, not because of your abilities, but because of your availability. When you organize your life around Jesus's top priority, you join the greatest movement in history.

You *become* part of something eternal.

This is the invitation: Follow Jesus. Be transformed. Help others do the same.

Conclusion: Living a Life Organized around Jesus's Priority

Simon Peter's journey with Jesus wasn't marked by perfection but by progression. He moved from self-interest to self-denial, from following at a distance to leading with boldness, from misunderstanding Jesus's mission to embracing it as his own. What changed? With the help of the Holy Spirit, Peter organized his life around Jesus's top priority.

That same invitation is extended to you.

You don't need to be a scholar, a pastor, or a spiritual expert. You just need to be someone who says yes. Yes, to surrender. Yes, to reordering. Yes, to investing in people. Yes, to following Jesus wherever he leads.

The world doesn't need more spectators. It needs more disciples who make disciples—ordinary people who live intentionally, love sacrificially, and point others to the One who changed everything.

Let's begin by asking ourselves what needs to shift in our lives so that Jesus's priority becomes central to us? Who might God be calling us to walk alongside as they grow in faith? What step will we take this week or even today to live as a disciple maker?

Peter's story is proof that God can use anyone who is willing. That includes you.

Don't wait for perfect conditions. Don't wait until you feel ready. Step out. Say yes. Organize your life around Jesus's top priority, and watch what he does through you.

This is your moment to *become*.

5 MAKE YOURSELF ACCOUNTABLE

Humans have a remarkable ability to adapt to physical stimuli. Scientists tell us that repeated exposure to a stimulus develops a diminished sensitivity to that stimulus. This phenomenon, known as sensory adaptation, explains why teenage boys who discover cologne sometimes apply too much. Over time their senses adapt, and they can no longer detect the smell, so they apply more. Before they realize it, too much of a good thing dominates the air space! The phenomenon of sensory adaptation can apply to many different stimuli, but the result remains the same. Repeated exposure to something often dulls our sensitivity to it.

Here's how I think this idea of sensory adaptation applies to our walk with Jesus. Many of us have spent time reading the New Testament or at least hearing stories preached and taught from it. Some of us grew up in children's church, where teachers offered stories about Jesus and the apostles. Later, youth leaders helped us apply the stories of faith to our adolescent angst. Perhaps we even today attend worship services or Bible studies built around the teachings of the Word.

The importance of the Bible to the Christian life can scarcely be overstated; however, the phenomenon of sensory adaptation applies here as well. The danger is that the stories of Jesus and his disciples become so familiar that they lose their influence over us.

A critical example of this scriptural sensory adaptation happens when we overlook the level of accountability practiced by first Jesus and the Twelve and later the early church. For our purposes here we should look at a few examples in Peter's life prior to Pentecost and then examine his Spirit-led growth.

Accountability in the Jesus Crowd

Mark records at least four clear examples of Peter being held accountable while following Jesus. This is important because Jesus modeled accountability as a necessary requisite to spiritual strength and practiced it in his relationship with his followers. As usual, Peter stands out, receiving Jesus's painful correction for all to see.

In Mark 8, Jesus asked the disciples the poignant question, "Who do you say I am?" (v. 27). Peter's resounding "You are the Messiah" (v. 29) might surprise us as readers. For a moment we all celebrate Peter's response, only to find him moments later the recipient of abrupt accountability. When Jesus explains his suffering, rejection, and death, Peter pulls him aside and rebukes him. Mark highlights the accountability of the Jesus community for us in Jesus's response: "'Get behind me, Satan!' he said. 'You do not have in mind the concerns of God, but merely human concerns'" (v. 33). Be sure to note that Jesus looked at the group when he said this to Peter (v. 33). Peter bore the brunt of the comment, but the others were meant to learn from his failure.

For Jesus, accountability in the context of his relationship with Peter provided the stinging yet necessary course correction for this leading apostle. I try to imagine Peter's expression when the same Jesus who called him from the nets now rebukes him in front of the others. Jesus isn't being harsh; he's demonstrating the kind of accountability that inspires growth. Most of us more easily forget the words of affirmation we hear than the words of correction. Sometimes we can rehearse word for word the interactions where someone holds us accountable. Peter experiences this from Jesus. Why this level of accountability? Jesus knows that Peter, the leading apostle, can't get this wrong. Jesus needs him to help guide the others.

This isn't the only example of Peter's accountability in Mark's Gospel. Mark 14 records three accountability examples. In a moment, we'll address Peter's unforgettable denial of Christ at Jesus's trial, but we can't overlook what happens just before. After the Last Supper and before Jesus's crucifixion, Jesus takes Peter, James, and John with him to Gethsemane (vv. 32-41). Jesus asks them to keep watch while he prays. Upon returning from prayer, Jesus finds Peter and the others asleep. Jesus corrects them and returns to praying, agonizing over obedience to the plan of redemption. Having invited them to now pray with him, twice more Jesus returns only to find Peter and the others asleep.

Fatigue is powerful, but as I read these texts, I find myself shaking my head. Peter, James, and John are the inner circle. These are the leaders of the Jesus community, and as Jesus agonizes over his impending death, they sleep. Three times they fail. Three times Jesus returns to hold them accountable. According to Luke's Gospel, these are the same disciples who asked Jesus to teach them to pray. Now, when the stakes are the greatest, they sleep and Jesus corrects them. The early church would eventually learn to value prayer, as we've noted. Perhaps this hard lesson in accountability provided the impetus for their eventual faithful practice.

The next scene again highlights Peter's passion and need for correction (vv. 47-50). Following the prayer in Gethsemane, Jesus is arrested, and upon the confrontation with his accusers, one of the disciples brandishes a sword and cuts off a soldier's ear. John 18 names Peter as the culprit. Jesus then says to Peter, "Put your sword away! Shall I not drink the cup the Father has given me?" (v. 11). In Peter's position, I might have done the same. Who wouldn't want to protect Jesus? Yet this kind of retaliatory violence had no place in Jesus's peaceable kingdom.

Peter's courtyard denial of Jesus in Mark 14 breaks our hearts. Upon Jesus's arrest and mock trial, Peter is compelled to be near Jesus. However, when the accusations turn in Peter's direction, he fails, denying Jesus three times. If we can overcome our sensory adaptation to this story, we experience the depths of Peter's despair. Not only has he failed his Lord, but Jesus is crucified, removing any perceived chance of Peter's reconciliation.

One of my favorite New Testament scenes occurs after the resurrection when Jesus finds Peter and the others once again toiling away at the nets. Peter, no doubt overwhelmed with the events of the last few days, has returned to fishing but not very successfully. Jesus calls out to the weary fishermen from the shore. I imagine that this kind of inquiry must have happened regularly. Curious bystanders or those who sold the fish must have tried to determine the daily fishing report from those on the water. Jesus instructs them to try the other side of the boat, and when they do, the catch is so great, they are unable to haul it in (John 21:6).

When Peter realizes that Jesus is the one calling, he dives in and swims to shore. We can't fully understand all that Peter is feeling, but he is compelled to get to Jesus. Perhaps in this too-good-to-be-true moment, he imagines apologizing to Jesus for his denial. These emotions are left to our imaginations.

After a breakfast around a warming fire, Jesus again holds Peter accountable for his actions, this time with three piercing refrains of "Do you love me?" (see vv. 15-17). Upon Peter's affirmative and gut-wrenching replies, Jesus drives home another critical issue. Jesus reminds Peter that to love him is to nurture those who will choose the Jesus way. We understand this is a kind of personal Great Commission for Peter.

Familiar stories all, but how often do we read them and fail to notice the value Jesus places on accountability for the Twelve? More than once, he interrupts their conversations only to reveal their prideful intentions or mistaken beliefs. Accountability was then, and is now, an essential component in spiritual growth and a critical practice as we become disciple makers in Jesus's name.

Near Capernaum in Mark 8, Peter's accountability clarifies who Jesus really is, even if he misunderstands Jesus's suffering. Here in John 21, Peter's accountability clarifies what Jesus asks of Peter, and ultimately all of us. Succinctly, if we love Jesus, we must love others and care for their relationship with Jesus. Accountability was an essential practice enabling the mission of Jesus to go forward.

Accountability in the Early Church

As we've noted, through the power of the Holy Spirit, Peter goes from denier to proclaimer on the day of Pentecost. What's more, he assumes a position of leadership in the birth of the early church. How remarkable to trace his journey, noting his failures, and then to see the impact of the Spirit's work as he now steps boldly into guiding the church in its infancy. What will emerge in the next few paragraphs reveals that accountability was also a hallmark of this early Christian community even after Jesus's resurrection and ascension.

On the day of Pentecost, we find Peter preaching with power. While his message celebrates the good news of Jesus Christ, it also confronts those who brought about his crucifixion.

> Fellow Israelites, listen to this: Jesus of Nazareth was a man accredited by God to you by miracles, wonders and signs, which God did among you through him, as you yourselves know. This man was handed over to you by God's deliberate plan and foreknowledge; and you, with the help of wicked men, put him to death by nailing him to the cross. (Acts 2:22-23)

Even with our tendency toward scriptural sensory adaptation, it's hard to miss the accountability Peter demonstrates in this message. Those who howled for Jesus's crucifixion must have scattered as Peter saddled them with the blame for his death. Those who resisted the urge to flee found in this moment of accountability the way to redemption. Scripture records that three thousand new believers were added on that day alone!

Later, as the church began to organize and the need for financial resources became apparent, many of the new believers sold their properties and gave the money to the ministry. Ananias and Sapphira, apparently members of this new Jesus movement, sold a piece of land and brought the money to the apostles. Acts 5 tells us that while they implied that the money was the full amount of the sale, they secretly held a portion of it back for themselves. Readers of Acts are astounded when their accountability, led by none other than Peter himself, results in their sudden deaths. An extreme case, to be sure; however, it highlights the seriousness of their spiritual fraud, attempting to fool the others into thinking they shared the same level of consecration and holiness. The credibility of the church was at stake, and their sin threatened the community formed by the Spirit around holiness and mission.

While Acts 10 records Peter's life-altering vision and the subsequent inclusion of the gentiles into God's mission (see ch. 1), Acts 11 demonstrates once again that the church didn't shy away from accountability. For centuries the rift between Jews and gentiles defined their relationship. So when God opened Peter's eyes and ultimately the doorway for gentiles to experience the saving grace of God, the fledgling church was understandably alarmed. Still very much a Jewish-themed faith, Christianity's global appeal hung in the balance as Peter explained his actions to the Jerusalem church (vv. 4-18). Even Peter, the leading apostle who had been with Jesus, had to give an account for this perceived breach of protocol. Thankfully, after hearing his explanation, the church rejoiced that even those long considered outsiders to the plans of God were now included in the Spirit-baptized community of believers. Accountability in the Acts church was the rule, not the exception.

We cannot overlook Acts 15 in this discussion of accountability as once again God's move to include the gentiles comes under the scrutiny of the church. The implications of this story are enticing, but a full examination of them will be reserved for another time. What's important for our purposes is to once again note that to be a believer in Jesus raised a person not only to new life but also to the kind of loving community that held its members accountable for their beliefs and actions. Peter, in Acts 15, now a bit more seasoned by Spirit-led leadership, offers to this debate, not thoughtless comments or a sword as in his earlier failures, but a wise compromise helping the church keep its arms wide open for the whole world.

The careful student of Acts might be anticipating a few comments about Galatians 2. While a bit outside our stated source material, it's difficult to address Peter's accountability without at least noting the conflict between Peter and Paul. Peter's vision and visit to Cornelius opened the door to the gentiles, but Paul, after his conversion, dove deep into a ministry to them. When Peter arrived in Antioch, where Paul had been ministering, Paul confronted him for shrinking back in his fellowship with the gentiles when Jews were present.

Readers long for a resolution to this story, but Paul doesn't offer any in Galatians. What we can affirm, however, is that Peter affirms Paul's mission to the gentiles in Acts 15, indicating his support for Paul, and later Peter refers to Paul as a "dear brother" in 2 Peter 3:15. Accountability was central to the ministry of the early church and its apostles. Let's turn now to the application of this essential principle to our becoming disciples and disciple makers.

Application

As a pastor I often included a section in my sermons simply titled "So What?" Preachers and writers love to retell the stories of God and offer their own theological perspectives, but the best sermons help us make practical applications of their content. This chapter on making ourselves accountable is no exception. Let's explore what all this talk of accountability means for those of us becoming disciple makers.

Joe[1] began to attend our church many years ago. He stood out from the crowd with his long hair, beard, and occasional exits to the sidewalk to smoke. He was delightful and kind, but his tattoos and general manner betrayed a checkered past.

1. Not actual name.

We began to meet for lunch at the taco truck. I found out he rode a motorcycle, so we rode some together, though we spent most of our riding time working on his bike. I discovered that Joe had only been out of prison for a few years. He had made a career of robbing Pizza Hut restaurants back in the days when they were all built alike. He knew just where to cut through the walls to gain access to the office and safe. He was no stranger to drugs and alcohol and eventually was caught, tried, and sentenced. His believing wife prayed him through the ordeal, and upon his release he came to faith in Christ. At the same time, Joe began faithfully attending Alcoholics Anonymous (AA) meetings.

Joe is still a friend and a leader in the church today. I won't forget a conversation we had. He said, "Sam, I like our church, and your preaching isn't bad. I have asked Jesus to forgive me, and he has, but the most powerful thing in my Christian life isn't your sermons. It's the reality that there are a dozen or so people at my AA meeting who know my story and would physically restrain me if I ever tried to drink and drug again. It is the power of those relationships that keeps me sober as much as anything." For a young pastor in my thirties, that testimony messed with my categories, but it has never left me. I think Joe learned from a difficult experience the power of accountability.

Elsewhere I have written more extensively on the subject of accountability, but I'm reminded of the story of the Apollo 11 lunar project. In 1962, President John F. Kennedy put the world on notice that America was going to the moon. In just seven short years astronaut Neil Armstrong stepped off a ladder and put the first human footprint onto the dusty lunar surface. A British Broadcasting Corporation study a few years ago revealed that the Apollo 11 project utilized the training and resources of four hundred thousand people! One person may announce a vision, another may take the first steps, but if we want to do extraordinary things, we need each other.

My friend Joe gives us a powerful message: If we want to do difficult things like break an addiction to alcohol or even go to the moon, we can't do it alone. We need each other.

The work of becoming disciple makers isn't easy. Anyone who has been moved by the call of the Great Commission can testify that knowing what we should do and actually doing it are two very different things. Understanding Jesus's mission of disciple making is easy, but doing it can feel daunting. This is where the power of making ourselves accountable comes into play.

Our culture has rediscovered the power of accountability. For a moment, stop and consider the places in our culture where accountability is championed. A little consideration reveals that various weight-loss programs, fitness models, educational cohorts, and recovery systems have rediscovered the power of being accountable to others. An African proverb applies here: "If you want to go fast, go alone. If you want to go far, go together."

I think this is the key to becoming disciple makers today. We need to come together with a small group of like-minded folks and hold one another accountable to Jesus's top priority. You might be wondering if something like this could ever work. I am happy to say it can; in fact, it has.

The Impact of John Wesley

Eighteenth-century Anglican pastor John Wesley is the famous founder of Methodism, but what's important to us in this instance is how he went about the founding of that movement. Wesley was a champion of accountability, weaving it into every element of his ministry. A full discussion of his methodology exists elsewhere, but suffice to say, to be a part of Wesley's class or band meetings meant subjecting yourself to accountability similar to what Jesus, his disciples, and the early church practiced. Wesley even had a phrase for it. He called it "watch[ing] over one another in love."[2] John Wesley himself credited this means of Christian community as the key element to the success of the early Methodist movement.

As we focus on becoming, we need accountability. Mountains of good intentions pile up around the Great Commission. Each of us reading this book wants to be faithful, and most of us have tried many times to take up Jesus's call. What we have likely overlooked is the power of loving accountability.

All of our efforts to *begin again*, to encounter the Holy Spirit, to *connect* with those people God has placed in our lives, and to *organize* our lives around Jesus's priority are extremely fragile if we don't gather some discipleship-minded friends around us and *make ourselves accountable* to them.

Imagine the potential of a small group of individuals meeting regularly with the purpose of watching over one another in love and encouraging one another in the work of making Christlike disciples in the nations. With God's help we might transform our discipleship efforts from crawling along in the dust to soaring to new heights. Accountability may be just what we need.

Application: The Courage to Be Known

Accountability isn't just about correction—it's about connection. It's about being known, challenged, and supported by a

2. John Wesley, "Advice to the People Called Methodists," in vol. 8 of *The Works of John Wesley*, 353.

community that shares your commitment to following Jesus. Peter's journey—full of bold declarations, painful failures, and Spirit-empowered growth—shows us that transformation is not a solo endeavor. It happens in the context of community, through loving truth-telling and mutual commitment to Christ.

What would happen if we stopped trying to follow Jesus in isolation? What if we embraced the humility to be known and the courage to be held accountable? Peter's story tells us that when we walk closely with others, Jesus can shape even our worst failures into fuel for mission.

So let's stop pretending that we can do this on our own. Let's stop hiding behind busyness, pride, or fear. Instead, let's step into the kind of community Jesus envisioned—a people who love one another enough to speak the truth, lift each other up, and call each other forward.

The mission is too important, and the stakes are too high, for us to settle for less.

A Helpful Example

In my book *A People of Grace: Becoming Disciples Together,* I defined the Covenant Formation Group as a practical and powerful expression of the church's call to "watch over one another in love," echoing the Wesleyan tradition. These groups are designed not only for personal growth but also to empower participants to become disciple makers themselves. A Covenant Formation Group is a structured, grace-saturated space where disciples are formed through relational commitment, spiritual practices, and mutual accountability.

Here are the key elements of the Covenant Formation Group. Perhaps something like this might help us *make ourselves accountable.*

1. **Intentional Commitment**: Members voluntarily commit to meet regularly for the purpose of spiritual formation and growth as disciples of Jesus.
2. **Covenant Relationship**: The group operates under a shared covenant—a mutual promise to pursue holiness discipleship together, to be honest, supportive, and accountable.
3. **Grace-Filled Accountability**: The group is not about judgment but about helping one another live faithfully. Members are encouraged to speak the truth in love, challenge one another when necessary, and celebrate progress in the journey of faith.
4. **Christ-Centered Focus**: Everything centers on becoming more like Jesus. Scripture, prayer, confession, and shared spiritual practices are tools to help members reflect Jesus in their daily lives.
5. **Transformation over Information**: The goal isn't simply learning more about the Bible but allowing God's Word and the Spirit-filled community to shape hearts, habits, and relationships.

Make yourself accountable, not because you're weak, but because you were never meant to walk this road alone. Like Peter, your story is still unfolding. And with the help of others who love Jesus and love you, it can be a story of growth, courage, and deep transformation—just the kind of story the world desperately needs to see.

6 ENGAGE

Chinese philosopher Lao-tzu is credited with saying, "A journey of a thousand miles begins with a single step." This phrase reminds us that no matter how intimidating something may seem, progress starts when we take action and do *something*, no matter how small. When we overcome fear and procrastination, momentum builds, and step-by-step we advance toward our goal. Beginning, taking action, or engaging is a critical step in *becoming*.

To experience the transformation Jesus wants for us, we must engage! It's time to move, not just consider all that we've learned. As we examine the life of Simon Peter one final time, we will find him repeatedly saying yes to Jesus and taking decisive action. While we frequently characterize Peter as a person who "acts first and thinks later," his impulsiveness hides heart-deep conviction. We can learn from Peter's actions. As we consider the elements of BECOME, let's not get overwhelmed, but trust that God's transformation unfolds one small, faithful step at a time.

Simon Peter Engaging

Mark 1: The Call

When Jesus called Andrew and Simon (Peter), Mark records that they left their nets "at once" (1:18). Given Mark's tendency to use this phrase in his Gospel, it's difficult to say exactly how this scene unfolded. But since Peter was the source for Mark's work, we can assume that Peter wanted Mark to convey that he followed Jesus right then and there. This isn't news to readers of the Gospel. We frequently hear this point emphasized in sermons as pastors press home the need for a personal decision to follow Jesus. What I'd like for us to notice here is what doesn't happen.

Given the relational, economic, and social impact of the decision to follow Jesus, we would not blame Peter if he offered Jesus some rational and legitimate reasons and excused himself from this invitation. He had responsibilities at home and to his extended family. Perhaps he should simply continue fishing and support Jesus financially? Or maybe, in a moment of self-reflection, Peter might have acknowledged his infamous temperament and chosen to step aside. What if the thought of walking away from what he had always known to follow a relatively unknown rabbi was just too overwhelming? There were literally dozens of reasons why Peter could have chosen to remain a fisherman. But he didn't. He engaged. He took a step of action.

Any one of these potential excuses feels familiar to me. It seems the work of God's Spirit in our hearts and minds is almost always accompanied by an instant stream of excuses, reasons why we couldn't possibly do the thing the Spirit is asking. Peter surely had similar thoughts, yet, upon hearing Jesus's call, Peter obeyed immediately—no excuses. Peter engaged.

Mark 8: The Confession

Jesus quizzed his closest companions on the cultural opinion of his identity: "Who do people say I am?" (8:27). They replied, "John the Baptist . . . Elijah . . . one of the prophets" (v. 28). Jesus pressed even deeper, asking the group, "But what about you? . . .

Who do you say I am?" (v. 29). The question barely escaped Jesus's lips when Peter replied, "You are the Messiah" (v. 29).

We expect Peter to speak first, but something more profound happens here. Peter appears to be the first of the disciples to grasp Jesus's true identity. He and Andrew were the first to follow. Now Peter demonstrates that he is the first to believe. Peter engages the mission of Jesus, leading the others to do the same.

Acts 1: Leadership in the Early Church

Following Jesus's ascension, we find the apostles gathered for prayer in the upper room where they were staying. Judas's betrayal of Jesus and subsequent death has left a vacancy among the Twelve. The text offers only a few clues, but apparently it has become clear to Peter that Judas's place must be filled. Acts 1:15 records that Peter took charge of the gathering and led those gathered through the process of discovering Judas's replacement.

Peter, first to follow, first to believe, is now engaging as the leader of the fledgling church. There is no procrastination in Peter, only engagement with the mission Christ has given, step-by-step leading the way.

Acts 2: Pentecost Preacher

Pentecost radically changed the way God interacted with humans. The gift of the Spirit to this point in Scripture was occasional, meaning that God gave the Spirit on certain occasions as God saw fit. For instance, Old Testament king David was filled with God's Spirit. The judges worked their famous deeds under the power of the Spirit. The prophets spoke as God's Spirit gave them utterance. But at Pentecost, God no longer worked only through designated leaders in specific circumstances; God decided to give the gift of the Spirit to every believer. God no longer interacted from a distance; the disciples no longer needed to clamor for the physical presence of Jesus. On the day of Pentecost, God established a new reality of intimacy with people: God was not just with but within every believer.

Acts 2 records that the gift of the Spirit resulted in the message of Jesus being proclaimed in multiple languages matching the nationalities of the people gathered. By now we might expect what happens in verse 14: "Then Peter stood up with the Eleven, raised his voice and addressed the crowd." As the Spirit prompted the need for preaching, Peter stepped up, proclaiming Jesus as the Messiah, and three thousand new believers were added to the church that day.

Following, believing, leading, and preaching, Peter models for us the importance of engaging the mission of Jesus.

Acts 3: Healing and Teaching

Jesus's ministry had been characterized by preaching, teaching, and healing. Acts 3 reveals Peter once again leading the way in engagement with the ministry of Jesus. When Peter heals a crippled beggar near the temple courts, he uses the occasion to boldly proclaim the power of Christ as the source for this miraculous sign.

At the Spirit's prompting, when the situation called for action, Peter stepped forward. Chapter by chapter we see Peter emerge as the leader of the Acts church.

Acts 10–11: Including the Gentiles

We've detailed this story already, so another detailed explanation isn't necessary. However, note again that at the Spirit's prompting, the spotlight shines on Peter, not for his procrastination or inactivity, but for his bold obedience. We marvel at his growth throughout these chapters: first to follow, first to believe, first to take leadership, first to preach, first to heal and teach, and now first to open the way to the gentiles. Imagine being present at such monumental moves of God. At the crucifixion, the resurrection, the ascension, Pentecost, and the gentile revival, Simon Peter stands front and center. God knew who to call on to lead the way in engaging the mission of Jesus.

Why Would Simon Engage?

What would cause a person to walk away from the security of the family business, follow with abandon an unproven rabbi, take the reins of a group whose leader had just been crucified, boldly proclaim the messianic identity of Jesus of Nazareth, and open the door to a people long considered second-class? I think the answer has the potential to energize our engagement with these aspects of BECOME.

Peter was no stranger to the teachings about God. Like all Jews in his era, he learned at the knee of his parents what would be strengthened in the synagogue. The story of God's perfect creation marred by sinfulness pointed repeatedly to humanity's need for a redeemer. Generation after generation watched and waited for the one who would come and do what Noah couldn't, what Moses couldn't, what the kings couldn't, and what the prophets foretold. Peter, Andrew, James, John, and all the other disciples believed that Jesus was that redeemer. Jesus's preaching, teaching, and miracles anchored their belief that God's Messiah was Jesus of Nazareth. So powerful was their experience of God's presence and power in the person of Jesus that they risked their whole lives in following Jesus. In our language, they were so convinced Jesus was the Christ that they took their lives out of neutral—simply looking to the eastern sky and waiting—and engaged with Jesus in the ministry of disciple making.

These disciples *became* something brand-new when they met Jesus, and we can too. In fact, I believe we must. The call of Jesus is too important for anything less than a full engagement in becoming disciple makers.

Application

A few years ago, some friends convinced me to take up rock climbing. In all transparency, I had no idea what I was getting into when I agreed to join them on a climb. We traveled to Oregon, drove serpentine logging roads deep into the forest, and hiked up a slippery trail carrying backpacks, rope, helmets, and harnesses. My first glimpse of the rock face made me seriously consider the sanity of my decision. But my friends were fanatical about safety and were patient teachers. By the second day, I was scaling the steeper surfaces with more confidence and scrambling up the gentler slopes with ease. When I phoned home to update my wife, she responded to my descriptions with, "Who are you? You're deathly afraid of heights!" She was right.

One afternoon, after having made the highest ascent of our trip, the most seasoned of the climbers declared that rather than climbing down the rock face, this time we would repel. Perched on a sloping ledge, he arranged our gear and gave us a thorough lesson in technique. Bolstered by my newfound confidence and quite ready to get back down to a less sloping and slippery ledge, I volunteered to go first.

I carefully listened as my friend gave me final instructions, and after a short prayer (no kidding), I stepped backward off the ledge, feeding the rope through my hands and harness. It wasn't perfect initially, but I soon got the hang of it and glided safely to the ground below.

It was one of the most exhilarating things I have ever done, but there was a moment, the moment when I said that little prayer, that I had to commit. I had to trust my guide, trust the equipment, and step back off the ledge.

Every significant thing we do has a moment when we commit. Sometimes it's stepping out to an altar of prayer; sometimes it's signing the adoption papers; sometimes it's dropping down on one knee to propose; sometimes it's saying yes to the cross-country job offer. Significant moments are always preceded by a "now or never," "go or no go," decision. Becoming is no different. Like Peter before us, there has to be a moment when we decide to engage.

This is that moment. You've read this far. You've evaluated the content of the acronym and tested the application to your life in Christ.

- **B** — You've seriously considered whether or not God is calling you to *begin again*, to make another effort at pursuing the Great Commission.
- **E** — You've spent time thinking about the apostle Peter and the transformation in his life due to his *encounter with the Holy Spirit*. You've whispered a prayer asking, "Lord, is there something more you long to do in me and through me?"
- **C** — You've taken an inventory of your *connections*. Who are the people already in your life? Is God nudging you to deepen your relationship with them?
- **O** — You've spent time evaluating your current schedule, noting the narrow margins. You've wrestled with the changes God might be asking of you so that you can *organize your life* to connect with neighbors, friends, classmates, or coworkers.

- **M** — You've crafted a little mental list of like-minded friends whom you might invite to *make you accountable* to this call to follow Jesus and include others on your journey of grace.
- **E** — Now, here you stand—helmet on, harness snug, rope in hand. The Guide is coaching you, and it's time to *engage*, to step off the ledge into one of the most exhilarating experiences of your life.

You can *become* a disciple of Jesus who joins with him in making disciples, just as he commissioned us in Matthew 28. But you have to engage. You have to start. Today's the day.

BECOME: Some Practical Action Steps

B — Begin Again

Pause long enough to reflect: "Is God calling me to recommit to the Great Commission?"

Action Steps

- Set aside time for prayer and reflection. Ask, "Lord, are you asking me to begin again?"
- Journal your spiritual journey: Are there areas of resistance to making disciples? What are they? Bring those hesitancies to Jesus, and let him speak to you about them.
- Renew your commitment to Jesus's mission with a simple, sincere prayer of surrender.

E — Encounter the Presence and Power of the Holy Spirit

Peter's transformation wasn't about trying harder but about being filled. Everything changed after Pentecost. Discipleship that makes disciples requires supernatural strength.

Action Steps

- Pray daily: "Holy Spirit, fill me and lead me today."

- Reflect on how the Spirit changed Peter, and ask God to do the same in you.
- Spend time in worship and silence, listening for God's presence and promptings.

C — Consider Your Connections

God often works through existing relationships. Who has he already placed around you?

Action Steps

- Make a list of five to ten people in your life—friends, neighbors, coworkers, family.
- Pray for each person by name. Ask God to open doors for deeper connection.
- Look for ways to serve, listen, and engage with gospel intentionality.

O — Organize Your Life

Following Jesus requires time and margin. Our calendars reveal our priorities.

Action Steps

- Audit your weekly schedule. Where is time being wasted or misprioritized?
- Do the hard work of creating space for relationships, ministry, rest, and reflection.
- Talk with your spouse, family, or housemates about how your home can be a place of mission.

M — Make Yourself Accountable

Discipleship is a team sport. We grow best when we're walking with others.

Action Steps

- Identify one or two spiritually mature people you trust. Ask them to regularly check in on your spiritual growth.
- Join (or start) a discipleship group that values obedience, vulnerability, and mission.
- Set goals and share them out loud. Invite others to help you follow through.

E — Engage Boldly

Now it's time to act. Discipleship isn't just internal—it's missional. Peter didn't stay in the upper room. He stepped into the streets with courage and purpose.

Action Steps

- Identify one person from your connection list and reach out this week. Start a spiritual conversation, share your story, or offer prayer.
- Say yes to a risk: lead a Bible study, invite someone to church, or serve someone sacrificially.
- Trust the Holy Spirit to guide your words and actions. The step of faith is where God moves.

You were made to BECOME. The journey starts now. One faithful step at a time. You don't need to have it all figured out. You just need to say yes, and take the next step.

CONCLUSION

We began this journey emphasizing the reality of change, even recognizing God's creative fingerprints in the process of our transformation. We also emphasized the need for change. Though Jesus was clear in his call for us to "go and make disciples," the church struggles to do it. As we've progressed through the meaning behind the BECOME acronym, we have discovered six practical steps we can take to embrace again Jesus's call and get started. Even as I write this conclusion, I'm praying for anyone who might read this book to take up this life-transforming challenge.

When our son was a toddler, we loved to teach him little songs designed to help him learn. One of his favorites was "Head and Shoulders, Knees, and Toes." The origins of the song are lost to history, but musical historians believe that it was passed from generation to generation by parents and teachers attempting to engage the minds and bodies of squirmy little ones. It seems to be one of those songs that, at least in America, nearly everyone knows.

Sometimes when I've been invited to share at a discipleship conference or seminar, I conclude my presentation and invite the congregation to stand for a closing song. In church groups, this manner of closing a service is common and people expect a song that engages with the content of the talk and a closing prayer. Sometimes in settings like this, we even have an open-altar time, inviting people to step forward and commit to a new experience with Jesus.

Lately, I've begun to use "Head and Shoulders, Knees, and Toes" as the concluding song. I usually set it up as a normal kind of closing invitation song and then surprise the group with this children's song. As soon as I start the song, people immediately join me. The group is surprised, wondering why in the world we would sing that song but happily willing to participate.

I invite them to sing along with me once or twice, and then, with puzzled expressions, they stare at me as I share something like this:

> You might be wondering why in the world we would sing "Head and Shoulders, Knees, and Toes" at the end of a discipleship talk. Here's why: We know in our heads that Jesus has called us to be and make disciples. We feel the weight of it on our shoulders as we have struggled to get it done. Today, it's time to hit our knees in prayer, asking for God's help, and get our toes moving in the direction of the people God has placed in our lives.

There's something about the familiarity of that little song when applied to the call to discipleship that impacts the hearts of the listeners. As crazy as it may sound, more than once we have invited people to a time of prayer and watched them come forward, asking God to help them change.

Do you believe you can *become* the kind of disciple who follows Jesus and includes others in your journey of grace? I believe you can because God is doing this work in me. If I can *become*, so can you.

I've been in the church all my life and a pastor for most of that time. I love Jesus and want to live in total obedience to him. But I've been bothered in my adult years by the Great Commission.

I know what Jesus meant, and I know it's for me, but I've struggled to make much progress.

Over the last decade or so, God has been helping me to discover the places in my life that crowd out his call and to take the necessary steps to change. The six steps in BECOME represent this course correction in my life.

I invite you to join with me and others as we follow Jesus and include others in our journey of grace, becoming like Christ and helping others do the same.

www.ingramcontent.com/pod-product-compliance
Lightning Source LLC
Chambersburg PA
CBHW060034050426
42448CB00012B/3009
* 9 7 8 0 8 3 4 1 4 3 9 8 2 *